The PENSION FUND REVOLUTION

Transaction Books by Peter F. Drucker

PETER F. DRUCKER

The PENSION FUND REVOLUTION

With a New Introduction and Epilogue by the Author

Transaction Publishers
New Brunswick (U.S.A.) and London (U.K.)

This book is printed on acid-free paper that meets the American National Standard for Permanence of Paper for Printed Library Materials.

Library of Congress Catalog Number: 92-5137
ISBN: 1-56000-626-9
Printed in the United States of America

Library of Congress Cataloging-in-Publication Data

Drucker, Peter Ferdinand, 1909-
    [Unseen revolution]
    The pension fund revolution / Peter F. Drucker ; with a new introduction by the author.
      p. cm.
    Originally published: The unseen revolution. 1st ed. New York : Harper & Row, c1976.
    Includes index.
    ISBN 1-56000-626-9
    1. Pension trusts—United States—Investments. 2. Corporations—United States—Finance. 3. Business enterprises, Trade-union—United States. I. Title.
    [HD7105.45.U6D78   1992]
    330.973′092—dc20
                                                   92-5137
                                                    CIP

Contents

Introduction to the Transaction Edition

No book of mine was ever more on target than *The Pension Fund Revolution* when it was first published (under the title *The Unseen Revolution*) in 1976. And no book of mine has ever been more totally ignored. It reported accomplished facts, but they were simply not acceptable to the 1976 *zeitgeist*. The book reported that institutional investors, especially pension funds, had become the controlling owners of America's large companies and, indeed, the country's only "capitalists." The shift had actually begun twenty-five years earlier with the establishment in 1952 of the first modern pension fund by General Motors. By 1960 it had become so obvious that a group of young men, meeting for the first time in my postgraduate seminar on innovation and entrepreneurship at New York University's Graduate Business School, had been persuaded by the seminar's discussions to found a stock-exchange firm catering exclusively to these new investors. Ten years later, by 1970, this firm, Donaldson, Lufkin & Jenrette, had already become the most successful and one of the biggest of Wall Street firms. Still, the conventional wisdom still held that the United States had become and would remain a country of "people's capitalism" with untold millions of individual shareholders owning the country's "means of production." That instead ownership had become highly concentrated in large institutional hands, and that through the pension funds "ownership of the means of production" had become "socialized" without becoming "nationalized," was simply unacceptable despite all the evidence. Indeed the financial crowd on Wall Street who were themselves then focusing their business more and more on these pension-fund investors pooh-poohed the book the most loudly.

Even less acceptable was the second theme of this book: the aging of America. That too, by 1976, had become an accomplished fact—the "baby bust" had, of course, started in 1961, a full fifteen years earlier; and the extension of life span well beyond traditional retirement age had started even earlier, in the early mid-1950s. But everybody in 1976 still believed in the "Youth Culture." Everybody still believed that "you can't trust anyone over thirty." Everybody still was convinced that the United States would for long years to come—perhaps forever—be dominated by adolescents and young adults, their values, their concerns, their "sincerity." Thus, the conclusions of this book—that a major problem was going to be the support of old people; that a major health-care issue would be longevity; that pensions and social security would be central to American economy and society; that retirement-age would have to be extended; and that altogether American policies would increasingly be dominated by middle-class issues and the values of old people—could not possibly be listened to.

And so there was only one positive review of this book. Kenneth Boulding, the distinguished economist and sociologist called me "a foremost philosopher of American society" in *The American Banker*. All the other reviews—and there weren't many—tore the book to shreds.

In a textbook case of Thomas Kuhn's "paradigm shift" the book then was "rediscovered" fifteen years later. In the late 1980s, it suddenly became "hot." Article after article—especially in the law reviews—now deals with the issues the book first presented and refers to it as a "classic." This reissue of the book by Transaction is thus timely—and I am grateful for it.

The book presented issues. It did not present solutions—least of all for its central concern: the impact of pension-fund ownership on the governance of the American corporation and on the structure of the American economy altogether. Fifteen years later—after two decades of financial and economic turbulence, of hostile takeovers and leveraged buyouts, of restructuring of companies everyone fifteen years ago thought as indestructible as the pyramids—with most of this, caused by the shift of ownership to the pension funds—we are beginning to see solutions. All the other books of mine in this Transaction series are being reissued as originally written, except for a new introduction to each. I still have not changed a word in the text of this book, but I am appending to it a 1991 article "The Governance of Corporations" that attempts to outline where we are going to come out, indeed where we already *are* coming out—and it is a greatly changed American economy with a greatly changed structure of management, of power, of control.

1. The Revolution No One Noticed

The Attainment of Pension Fund Socialism

If "socialism" is defined as "ownership of the means of production by the workers"—and this is both the orthodox and the only rigorous definition—then the United States is the first truly "Socialist" country.

Through their pension funds, employees of American business today own at least 25 percent of its equity capital, which is more than enough for control. The pension funds of the self-employed, of the public employees, and of school and college teachers own at least another 10 percent, giving the workers of America ownership of more than one-third of the equity capital of American business. Within another ten years the pension funds will inevitably increase their holdings, and by 1985 (probably sooner), they will own at least 50—if not 60—percent of equity capital. Ten years later, or well before the turn of the century, their holding should exceed around two-thirds of the equity capital (that is, the common shares) plus a major portion—perhaps 40 percent—of the debt capital (bonds, debentures, and notes) of the American economy. Inflation can only speed up this process.

Even more important especially for Socialist theory, the largest employee pension funds, those of the 1,000–1,300 biggest companies plus the 35 industry-wide funds (those of the college teachers and the teamsters for instance) already own control* of practically every single one of the 1,000 largest industrial corporations in America. This includes control of companies with sales well below $100 million, by today's standards at best fair-sized companies, if not actually small; the pension funds also control the fifty largest companies in each of the "non-industrial" groups, that is, in banking, insurance, retail, communications, and transportation.† These are what Socialist theory calls the "command positions" of the economy; whoever controls them is in command of the rest.

Indeed, aside from farming, a larger sector of the American economy is owned today by the American worker through his investment agent, the pension fund, than Allende in Chile had brought under government ownership to make Chile a "Socialist country," than Castro's Cuba has actually nationalized, or than had been nationalized in Hungary or Poland at the height of Stalinism.

In terms of Socialist theory, the employees of America are the only true "owners" of the means of production. Through their pension funds they are the only true "capitalists" around, owning, controlling, and directing the country's "capital fund." The "means of production," that

---

*That is, they own at least one-third.

†The only exceptions are a few government-owned businesses, such as TVA; farmer-owned producer cooperatives like Sunkist Oranges; policy-holder-owned "mutual insurance companies," such as Prudential and most of the other very large life-insurance companies; and a shrinking group of smaller firms, in which the founders or their immediate descendants still either own the entire business or control it.

is, the American economy—again with agriculture the only important exception—is being run for the benefit of the country's employees. Profits increasingly become retirement pensions, that is, "deferred compensation" of the employees. There is no "surplus value"; business revenue goes into the "wage fund."

Other countries have been moving in similar directions. The first charge on big business in Japan is job and income security for its employees. This is what "lifetime employment" means in terms of economic structure. If employees cannot be fired except when a business is bankrupt, then maintaining employee jobs and employee income must be the overriding demand on business management; job security rather than profit becomes the firm's objective and the test of management performance. But there is no trace in the Japanese system of "employee ownership," let alone of ownership and control of the nation's "capital fund" by either the employees or their trustees.*

At the opposite end of the spectrum of modern economies is Yugoslavia. There the workers or their representatives control the enterprise in which they are employed, elect its management, serve as a review board for that management, and can remove individual managers (though they cannot abolish management, the management function, or even management positions). Yet the workers have no say whatever about the formation, supply, or allocation of capital, which remains a tightly controlled state monopoly. Yugoslav workers, unlike Japanese workers, manage the means of production. But they do not control them, nor are the means of production run for their benefit. On the contrary, the state exacts a very heavy "cost of capital";

*On this, see my paper "Economic Realities and Enterprise Strategy," in *Modern Japanese Organization and Decision-Making,* edited by Ezra F. Vogel (Berkeley: University of California Press, 1975).

what Marxists call "surplus value" accrues to a "state capitalist fund" rather than to the "wage fund." The workers get bonuses if the company does well. If it does poorly, on the other hand, they lose their jobs and have no guaranteed pension bought for them out of past company revenues.

Only in the United States do the employees both own and get the profits, in the form of pensions, as part of wage income. Only in the United States are the employees through their pension funds also becoming the legal owners, the suppliers of capital, and the controlling force in the capital market.

In terms of nineteenth-century political economy—and especially Marxist theory—Yugoslavia is "state capitalism" rather than a form of "socialism," though its capitalism is tempered by a high degree of local worker autonomy and worker responsibility. Japan is a "finance capitalism," with privately owned and independently managed banks making the ultimate capital-allocation decisions, though this is a finance capitalism subject to stringent safeguards on workers' jobs and workers' income. The United States alone, in terms of economic structure, has made the final step to a genuine "socialism," in which (to use Marxist terminology) "labor" as the "source of all value" receives the "full fruits of the productive process."

In other words, without consciously trying, the United States has "socialized" the economy but not "nationalized" it. America still sees herself, and is seen elsewhere, as "capitalist"; but if terms like "socialism" or "capitalism" have any meaning at all, the American system has actually become the "decentralized market socialism" which all the Marxist church fathers, saints, and apostles before Lenin had been preaching and promising, from Engels to Bebel and Kautsky, from Viktor Adler to Rosa Luxemburg, Jaurès, and Eugene Debs.

Socialism came to America neither through the ballot box nor through the class struggle let alone a revolutionary uprising, neither as a result of "expropriating the expropriators" nor through a "crisis" brought on by the "contradictions of capitalism." Indeed, it was brought about by the most unlikely revolutionary of them all—the chief executive officer of America's largest manufacturing company, General Motors. Twenty-six years ago, in April 1950, Charles Wilson, then GM's president, proposed the establishment of a pension fund for GM workers to the United Automobile Workers Union. The UAW was at first far from enthusiastic, even though by that time pensions had become a priority demand of the American union movement. The union leaders saw clearly that Wilson's proposal aimed at making the pension system the business of the private sector. And the UAW—in common with most American unions—was in those years deeply committed to governmental social security. Wilson's proposal gave the union no role whatever in administering the General Motors pension fund. Instead, the company was to be responsible for the fund, which would be entrusted to professional "asset managers."

The union feared, with good reason as subsequent events have proven, that the pension fund would strengthen management and make the union members more dependent on it. Wilson's major innovation was a pension fund investing in the "American economy"—in other words, the free-enterprise system. And while this made financial sense to the union leaders, their strong preference until then had been for pension funds invested in government securities, that is, in the public sector. The union leadership was greatly concerned lest a company-financed and company-managed private pension plan—negotiated with the union and incorporated into the collective bargaining agreement—would open up a conflict within the union membership between older workers, interested in the largest possible pension payments, and younger workers, interested primarily in the cash in their weekly pay envelope. Above all, the union realized that one of the main reasons behind Wilson's proposal was a desire to blunt union militancy by making visible the workers' stake in company profits and company success. (One of the stalwarts in the GM department of the UAW proposed at that time, in all seriousness, that the union should lodge an unfair labor practices complaint against Wilson, since his pension proposal could have no purpose except to undermine the union.) But Wilson's offer was too tempting, especially to the rapidly growing number of older workers in the UAW. And so, in October 1950, the GM Pension Fund began to operate.

Employee pension funds in American industry go back to the Civil War, if not beyond it. By 1950, there were some 2,000 in operation. One of them, that of the Bell Telephone System, was already very large and is still bigger than that of any other company and of most governmental units. Employee pension plans, therefore, were far from being a novelty at the time. Nor was the idea of making the pension plan part of the labor contract particularly startling. Indeed, a few months before Wilson announced his proposal the Supreme Court had ruled, in a case involving the Inland Steel Company, that employers had to bargain about pensions with their unions. And the Internal Revenue Service had much earlier decided to treat business contributions to employee pension plans as legitimate and deductible expenses for tax purposes.

Wilson's timing was influenced by these developments. But he had been planning his proposal for a very long while and was only waiting for the propitious moment, when events would make his associates in GM management willing to support such "heretical" ideas. Indeed, he first mentioned to me his conviction that workers had to have a company-financed pension plan in a conversation in the spring of 1944, toward the end of World War II. Even then he had obviously given a good deal of time and thought to the subject, and wanted to know my reaction to a number of carefully thought-out alternatives. He probably worked out his final plan soon after the end of World War II, four or five years before he offered it to the union.

Both because of its innovative approach and its timing, the GM plan had totally unprecedented impact. Within one year after its inception, 8,000 new plans had been written —four times as many as had been set up in the 100 years before. Every single one of the new plans copied GM's one radical innovation, which has since been written into most of the older company plans as well. The GM plan was to be an "investment trust"; it was to invest in the capital market, and especially in equities. Practically all earlier plans had been "annuity" plans, to be invested in standard life-insurance investments such as government bonds, mortgages, and other fixed-interest-bearing instruments. The Bell System fund, for instance, had for decades been invested exclusively in U.S. Government bonds earning minimal interest.

Wilson rejected this for several reasons. He considered it financially unsound, indeed impossible, for a pension system embracing more than a small group of workers to be based on debt obligations alone. This, he thought, would either place an unbearable debt burden on the country and its industry, or force interest rates down so low as to cut drastically into workers' pension expectations. A broad-based pension plan had to "invest in America"—in her productive assets and her capacity to produce and to grow.

But Wilson also came to reject the strongly advocated

alternative to an annuity plan: a plan investing workers' pension fund monies in the company they worked for. Wilson genuinely believed in creating employee ownership of American business. Yet the traditional proposal—which incidentally Wilson's colleagues in GM top management strongly favored—struck him as financially unsound and incompatible with the workers' needs and interests. "The pension fund that puts its assets into buying the shares of the employing company puts all the worker's eggs into one basket," he argued. And the fewer eggs one has, the more careful one must be with them. Investing the worker's main savings in the business that employs him may be "industrial democracy," but it is financial irresponsibility. The employee already has a big stake in the company that employs him: his job. The job is the financial present. To put the employee's financial future, his pension claim, into the same "basket" violates all principles of sound investment.

Furthermore, it is financially dishonest. Under the guise of looking after the employee, the employee's wage—for pension money is "deferred wage"—is used to finance the "boss," the employing company. While masquerading as "industrial democracy" it is, in effect, a subsidy to the employing company and a crutch to its management. No matter how poorly it performs, it has a ready pool of capital at its disposal to bail it out (as twenty-five years after Wilson, in 1975, the pension funds of New York City employees were used to bail out their employer, New York City, and its incompetent and irresponsible management). Above all, as Wilson pointed out, to use employee pension money to invest in the employing company would make sure that few employees would ever get a pension. Over a period of thirty or forty years—the time needed to build up a decent pension—the great majority of existing companies and industries go downhill; indeed, in a forty-year period more than half of all businesses, large and small, disappear altogether. Where, Wilson asked, would the anthracite coal miners be under "industrial democracy"? Theirs had been the most profitable American industry as recently as 1925, only to vanish fifteen years later.

Anyone in the United States making this point, especially around 1950, was immediately told to look at the Sears Roebuck profit-sharing pension fund, which since its inception in 1916 had invested almost entirely in Sears Roebuck stock and had done so well that long-serving rank-and-file workers, janitors in a store for instance, retired in the forties and fifties as wealthy men. Wilson had a ready answer: a chart showing how the employees of other major American retail companies doing well in 1916 would have fared had their employers then adopted the same plan as Sears. More than half of the leading retailers of 1916 had disappeared by 1950, thirty-five years later—a good many of them even before the depression. And the surviving companies, including such well-known names as Montgomery Ward, J. C. Penney, or the A. & P., had done so poorly on average that employees dependent for their pensions on funds invested in these companies would, in 1950, have had to retire with little or no retirement income. The outcome would have been the same had the Ford Motor Company in the years of its meteoric rise before World War I adopted a profit-sharing pension plan to be invested in Ford Company stock, as Henry Ford once thought of doing before he was persuaded instead to triple the minimum wage to $5 a day in 1913–14. By the time the first Ford workers had reached retirement, their pension claims would have been nearly worthless; for by the mid-twenties, despite a booming automobile market, the Ford Motor Company had ceased to be profitable and had entered a rapid decline that was not reversed until twenty years later, after World War II. And it is anything but certain that Sears employees going to work for the company now, in the mid-seventies, will fare anywhere near as well when they reach retirement age as their predecessors who joined the company fifty years ago.

Wilson thus rejected a pension plan tied to the fortunes of the employee's own company. Such a plan may make the employees "owners"; but it also means that they cannot count on a pension and, indeed, that half of them will get no pension. It is far less an "employee benefit plan" than an "employer" or "management" benefit plan. Equally, he rejected an "annuity" plan as fundamentally unworkable. Pension claims are claims to future income; but if everyone is under a pension plan—an outcome Wilson fully expected —the burden of such a mountain of fixed obligations becomes unbearable. Pension plans had to be based on ownership in productive resources rather than on debt claims against them. And such ownership had to be in the country's productive capacity rather than in a particular company, and to be managed professionally and flexibly, as "investment," which could be drawn out from a company or industry with poor prospects and put where prospects were best for earnings and capital gains. Whether Wilson knew it or not, this conclusion committed the United States to pension fund socialism.

In any case, Wilson prevailed. His four basic rules for pension fund investment—professional independent management of corporate pension funds as "investment funds"; minimal or no investment in the company for which the employee works; no investment in any company in excess of 5 percent of the company's total capital; and no investment in any company of more than 10 percent or so of the total assets of the pension fund—were finally written into the country's laws in the 1974 Pension Reform Act.*

• • •

A NOTE ON TERMS: In discussing pensions and pension funds, five terms are commonly used: (1) *Vesting.* This means that the participating employee, usually after a number of years (with ten years the maximum for private pension plans under ERISA) acquires a "vested interest" in a pension payable when he reaches retirement age, i.e., sixty-five or, in some plans, sixty. He cannot draw out the money until then, borrow against it or, as a rule, assign or sell his interest. But if he reaches retirement age he is assured of a pension even if he quits, is laid off, or stops contributing for any reason. The term that corresponds to "vesting" in ordinary life insurance is "the paid-up value" of an insurance policy. (2) *Funding.* This means building up actuarially adequate reserves, based on actuarial assumptions on life expectancy of the participants, on interest rates, and on future pension levels. In insurance terms, these are the "policy reserves." (3) *Past-service liabilities.* This is the funding obligation for the pension claims of employees who were already on the payroll when the pension fund started, and who under most contracts are entitled to a full pension even though, of course, nothing was paid into the fund for them in earlier years. Every increase in pension benefits—because wages go up, for instance—creates a new set of "past-service liabilities" for employees already on the payroll which, under ERISA, have to be "funded" over a period of years. (4) *Death benefits* are the amounts payable—under many, though by no means all, private pension contracts—to the employee's heirs should he die before he begins to draw his pension. (5) *The guaranteed payment period*

*The full name is Employees Retirement Security Act, ERISA, an act quite as unwieldy as its name suggests.

—again not provided for in many contracts—is a contractual guarantee of ten, fifteen, or (rarely) twenty years of pension payments whether the pensioner survives or not. ERISA made mandatory for all private pension funds the first three: vesting, funding, and funding of past-service liabilities.

● ● ●

By now there are some 50,000 or so pension plans in existence in America. Practically all of them are "investment funds," whether they are being managed, like the GM plan, by a separate professional full-time staff of their own; by professional "asset managers," above all by the trust departments of the big banks (the largest number); or by insurance companies. At the end of 1974, the pension funds of the 1,000 or so largest companies had about $115 billion in assets; large industry-wide and mainly union-managed pension funds had about $35 billion; and the non-business pension funds (other than those of federal-government employees) about $50 billion. In addition there are the rapidly growing pension funds of the self-employed (the so-called Keogh plans) and the still quite new Individual Retirement Accounts (IRAs) of employees of companies which do not have a company pension plan.

Around 70 percent of the assets of these plans are invested in equities, that is, in shares of listed publicly-owned American companies. This gives a pension fund portfolio of at least $140 to $150 billion at the end of 1974 as against a list price of all companies traded on the stock market of about $500 billion at that time, or roughly 30 percent of the total value of the listed companies. Keogh plans and Individual Retirement Accounts hold together another 5 percent or so. Each year the pension funds take in about $20 billion more than they pay out, which means that they have to find investment for $20 billion a year. Social Security, by

contrast—while its total intake and outgo are much larger
—now operates at a cash deficit.

Newspaper stories in the next few years may report the
"folding" of a good many pension plans, but this will be an
optical illusion. In fact, both the number of plans and the
number of people covered by them will go up sharply. It is
true that a good number of small-company plans will
"fold"—in part because the Pension Reform Act of 1974
demands too much of them; in larger part, however, because the act gives small-company employees more, and
more advantageous, options to build their own IRA retirement plans at less cost and with higher tax benefits. What
looks like the collapse of a small-company plan is therefore
more likely to mean a shift to a different plan with better
tax treatment—an IRA. And small-company plans, while
numerous, cover only a tiny fraction of the country's employees.

The number of self-employed people building their own
pension plans (the so-called Keogh plans) is already growing explosively. The 1974 Pension Reform Act made these
plans particularly attractive; legally they are individual accounts, but by and large, their assets are managed and
invested like the assets of large corporate plans.* Above all,
the large pension funds will speed up their growth far faster
than the enrollments and assets of the small plans could
possibly decrease. The 1974 Pension Reform Act alone
made sure of that, by forcing private employers with pension plans to bring substantially all their employees under
pension plan coverage, and after a relatively short period
of employment. In certain companies, especially medium-

*The analogy is between group life insurance—corresponding to the corporate
pension plan—and individual life insurance, which corresponds to a Keogh Plan
Fund. The same insurance company writes both group-life and individual-life
policies. They differ contractually; but the premium reserves for both are invested
and managed exactly the same way.

sized ones, enrollment will thus go up sharply even in a period of low employment—sometimes by as much as 40 to 50 percent.

The Pension Reform Act further required that all private, non-governmental funds be brought up to stringent actuarial standards within a few years. For most companies this will mean at least five to ten years of sharply higher payments into their pension plans. Where pension fund contributions in the sixties and early seventies took about 20 percent of pre-tax earnings, by the late seventies and early eighties they will take 40 percent to handle actuarial obligations, and particularly "unfunded past service" obligations for employees already on the payroll. At the same time inflation has been pushing up wages and with them pension benefits, which again calls for larger employers' pension fund contributions. Pensions are normally based on the retiring employee's wage income during his last years of employment. Even the fund that was in full actuarial balance will thus be forced into an actuarial deficit position by inflation; contributions into the fund by the employer will have to be increased correspondingly. The larger private pension funds which together account for nine-tenths of total private pension fund enrollment—and probably for an even larger proportion of private pension fund assets— are therefore bound to grow at a fast rate even if the economy performs poorly.

Pension fund enrollment, pension fund assets, and pension fund ownership are bound to grow *faster* in this country over the next ten years (through the mid-eighties) than at any time since they started their fantastic growth in 1950. Such a growth rate staggers the imagination: enrollment during the last twenty-five years has doubled every seven years and assets every five years; yet that is the minimum rate to be expected through the mid-eighties.

This means, first, that the number of people covered by private pension plans (plans other than Social Security) is bound to grow much faster than the work force. In 1973, the year before the Pension Reform Act, about 30 million non-governmental employees, some 2 to 3 million self-employed people, and practically all employees of governments (around 15 million more) were covered by pension plans—for a total of almost 50 million out of an employed work force of 85–90 million. By 1985, the number covered by pension plans will be up to at least 65 million, maybe even 70 million, out of a labor force at work of no more than 95 million (at a rate of 96 percent of labor-force employment, which is the legal definition of "full employment" in the United States). More than two-thirds of all working people in America, employed or self-employed, will be covered by a pension plan in addition to Social Security. Pension plan coverage will then be more nearly universal than life insurance, and as common as provision is today for hospital and medical expenses through all the various payment mechanisms (Blue Cross, Blue Shield, private health insurance, Medicare, Medicaid, Armed Services, Veterans, etc.).

In the past twenty-five years pension fund assets have doubled every five years. Until the mid-eighties these funds will continue to grow at least at this rate (and faster if inflation continues). They will not reach a balance, with annual income roughly equaling annual outgo, until the early nineties, although their growth should slacken sharply after 1985. But between now (1976) and 1985 the assets of the private pension funds alone will reach at least $300 billion.* With 70 percent of these assets invested in equity capital of listed corporations—the historical ratio—

*At the 1976 value of the dollar.

the pension funds of the employees of American business will by themselves own 50 percent of that business by 1985. The pension funds of the self-employed and the Individual Retirement Accounts (IRAs) may by then own another 10 percent, indeed 15 percent is not at all improbable; and the pension funds of government employees might own another 5 to 10 percent. This amounts to a minimum of 50 percent and a "most probable" of 65 to 70 percent of equity ownership by the pension funds within the next ten or fifteen years. In other words, pension funds will "own" America by then, except for the agricultural and governmental sectors; and they will be a main source of finance for these sectors too.

True, economic fluctuations may modify this timetable. A genuine long-term depression might actually speed it up, as employment (and with it pension contributions) tends to go down less sharply in a depression than stock prices. But only continuous double-digit inflation lasting another decade or so could seriously change matters. While inflation is likely to erode and may even destroy the value of the benefits to the pensioners, it will not affect to any significant extent the pension funds' enrollment, their asset build-up, or their ownership position.

Unfinished Pension Fund Business

One more thing is predictable about the next ten years. During that time we will have to tackle the unfinished pension fund business facing the United States: that of the union-dominated, "industry-wide" pension funds and the pension funds of states, counties, cities, and other local governments.

When Congress discussed pension reform in the early

seventies, it talked a great deal about abuses. But the act that was finally passed and widely proclaimed as the means to stop these "abuses" only codified, and then festooned with a great deal of red tape, the practices of the pension funds of the country's leading large companies—in respect to the rights of participants, the investment policies and the responsibilities of pension fund managements, and so on. The two major requirements of the Pension Reform Act: the vesting of pension rights after a maximum of ten years of employment, and the funding of pension claims, had been normal practices for large-company pension plans all along. For perhaps four out of every five participants in corporate pension plans, the Pension Reform Act thus made little practical difference.

The only innovation was something which many pension fund managers had been proposing for a long time:* compulsory government reinsurance against the risk of pension fund failure because a company goes bankrupt or out of business. Congress, in effect, said to the small companies, "Your pension plan must be brought up to the standard the big companies have developed. For the plans of the big companies are working and are performing."

There *is* unfinished business; but it is not in respect to the private pension plans with which Congress was so concerned in the 1974 act. There are two other kinds of pension funds—the union-dominated (or union-run) ones and those of states, counties, and local governments—which together account for a third or so (about 17 out of a total of 50 millions) of all employees covered by pension plans other than Social Security. Both kinds are in deep trouble and both are badly in need of reform.

*I myself originally proposed it as early as 1950; even then it was not considered particularly startling.

The union-dominated funds* usually started back in the 1920s or 1930s, well before the corporate pension funds got going. The Railroad Retirement Board dates back to World War I. These funds are usually "industry-wide"—that is, they cover people engaged in a profession such as college teaching, or in a craft such as construction workers or teamsters, people who, while they normally spend long years in the same profession or trade, also normally work for several employers.

There is nothing intrinsically wrong with industry-wide pension funds. Indeed, the largest of them, the Teachers Insurance and Annuity Association (TIAA), which, since the twenties, has provided pension coverage for faculty members and other employees of non-profit institutions, has an enviable record of performance as well as of innovation. But the "union-dominated" industry-wide pension fund tends to be grossly underfunded—the *cause célèbre* being the fund of Hoffa's Central States Teamsters Conference, headquartered in Chicago, with assets of almost $2 billion.† Labor leaders, understandably, do not like to increase the pension fund contributions of their members but prefer to pretend that pensions "come free." Worse still, in far too many cases these funds are deeply corrupt, with investments sometimes in the shadiest ventures, such as Las Vegas gambling casinos, second mortgages on real-estate speculation on marginal resort land, or projected "entertainment parks" 50 miles from nowhere, sometimes in partnership with known underground figures who have long criminal records. The money may go to union leaders

---

*I say "union-dominated" rather than "union-run" because one of the most important of these funds, the Railroad Retirement Act, is legally an agency of the U.S. government, even though the Railroad Brotherhoods have, from the beginning, had a decisive voice in its administration.

†For the sordid details of this fund, see *The Wall Street Journal,* July 22, 23, and 24, 1975.

or their cronies, and exorbitant fees are being paid to union officials and members of their families for services of no or dubious value.

Officially, these funds do come under the provisions of the Pension Reform Act of 1974. They are supposed to have independent trustees and to conform their investment policy to stringent rules which would exclude a good many of their worst investments. And they are supposed to disclose their records and their deals. But so far this is largely dead letter. In a few isolated cases the Department of Labor, which administers the act, has insisted on the removal of trustees who, contrary to the new act, have criminal records. Otherwise the Department is pleading lack of money as the reason for its failure to concern itself with the union-dominated funds. It is likely that only a scandal of mammoth proportions (the bankruptcy of one of these funds as a result of being looted by its trustees, for instance) will produce the political will to tackle what for years has been a festering and stinking sore. In the meantime, the participants in these funds—teamsters, in particular, but also coal miners and a good many construction workers—receive pitiful pensions. The remedy (to apply to the union-dominated funds those minimum standards long prevailing for corporate pension funds) is now on the statute books; however, it has still to be applied.

The second problem, that of the funds for government employees (and especially state and local government employees), is far more serious. And these funds cover more people than the labor-dominated ones—a total of nearly 15 million workers, or one-sixth of the U.S. labor force.

The pension funds for governmental employees are not controlled or regulated by law or by regulatory agencies of any kind; yet many are in far worse shape than even the most mismanaged labor-dominated plans. Very few governmental units have even attempted to fund their pension liabilities. Technically, these funds are insolvent. The most visible case of course is New York City. The fact that the pension liabilities which New York assumed, especially under the Lindsay administration, have so far not been funded, made it possible for the City to pretend for ten years that it "balanced its budget." And the fact that this illusion could no longer be maintained was the main reason —far more important than the erosion of the tax base, the high welfare load, or even the size of individual pension benefits promised to City employees—why the City went broke in 1975. Then it had to begin to meet the costs of increasing retirements without having provided for them in the years past. New York is however only the most visible case. Very few governmental pension funds (including those of the federal government) have funded their pension liabilities any better. All of them will have to use an increasing share of their revenues to catch up on pension liabilities already due, even if they cut pension promises sharply.

Many governmental units—the State of Florida, Boston, Indianapolis, and Pittsburgh are among the larger ones— have not funded their pension obligations at all. In other words, they have not laid aside one penny for future pension payments. To bring their funds up to the minimum acceptable for private pensions would mean increasing pension contributions by 50 percent or more for ten years —from about 40 cents for every dollar of state or city payroll to 60 cents or so, which would require proportionate increases in taxes and tax revenues. The alternative is an even steeper increase only a few years later, or the insolvency of the state or city governments and the repudiation of pension obligations to retiring and retired employees. In Pittsburgh, which has an unfunded pension fund liability of over $250 million, the state insurance commission has already declared the pension plan to be "in very critical condition"—the last step before a formal verdict of insolvency.

Even those local governments that do have funding programs tend grossly to underfund. Detroit pays a larger proportion of its tax revenues into the city's pension funds than any other big American city: 55 percent of city employees' wages. Yet these funds—largely as a result of sharp increases in both wages and pension benefits during the last ten years—have a past unfunded liability of over $1 billion.

The unfunded past-service liability of New York City's pension funds is "officially" estimated at $5.5–6 billion! Actually the figure is a good deal higher, though no one knows how much higher. For New York City bases its pension funds on actuarial computations made in 1918, when the average life expectancy of an employee was still well under fifty-five, as compared with well over seventy today. New York's pension contributions and reserves do not make any provision whatever for the ten to fifteen years of additional pension the City will have to pay to retired employees over and above the assumed pension fund liability. Some experts put New York City's unfunded past-service liability as high as $10 billion. And even the officially admitted $6 billion figure gives the City an unfunded past-service liability to its pension funds that is *larger* than all its bonds and notes in the hands of the public. Yet "unfunded past-service liability" is a debt like any other. Until New York City tackles the debt to its pension funds, all talk about "balancing New York City's budget" is gross dishonesty, and all plans to "salvage the City financially" are mockery.

It is popularly assumed that the problems of costs and of funding local government employees are problems of the big city. But this is simply not true. Small local governments, in many cases, have just as badly escalated pension promises and are just as far behind in funding. In Lancaster, Pennsylvania, a city of only 50,000, the pension funds of the policemen and firemen alone are underfunded to the tune of $10 million—$200 for each man, woman, and child in the city, or almost $1,000 per family. Yet Lancaster, in the heart of the Amish country, is considered a paragon of financial conservatism.

The pension funds of state, county, and city governments are equally in need of managerial reform. Many governmental pension funds throughout the nation have high costs, an abysmal investment record, and a long tradition of management by political crony. That the Comptroller of New York State is the *sole* trustee for the pension funds of the state's employees, accountable to no one, is fairly typical; such an arrangement would never be tolerated for a private pension fund, no matter how estimable the individual.

Governmental pension funds need to be put under the ERISA provisions in respect to vesting, to funding, to past-service pension liabilities, and to management. At the very least this will bring the problems out into the open. It will not prevent "crises"; indeed, it will show that many governmental units—perhaps most—are in deep financial trouble. But it will prevent both the financial skullduggery that enabled New York City to cover up its crisis until the City was bankrupt and the "sudden surprise" when the day of reckoning can no longer be postponed.

The basic problem of the governmental pension funds is however neither financial nor managerial. It is the "involuntary servitude" they impose on governmental employees, which approaches a form of peonage. The fact that this was not "planned," and is largely the result of pressures exerted by the employees' own unions, does not make it any the less incompatible with justice, individual freedom, and social mobility, nor any less undesirable for employer and employee alike as well as for the tax-paying citizen.

Not many governmental pension funds provide retirement pensions as lush as those of New York City or San Francisco, which may run 50 or 60 percent higher than private pensions and can, if the employee plays it right, equal or even exceed the highest salary he earned during his working career. But altogether the majority of government employees, including federal employees, are entitled to substantially larger pensions than the corporate pension plans provide. Most governmental employees also enjoy very large early retirement pensions, e.g., 60 percent of the maximum pension (or 40 percent plus of their highest annual income) after twenty or twenty-five years of service. The rapid escalation of pension benefits in governmental employment has been a major cause of the explosive rise in government (and especially local government) costs these last fifteen years.

But local and state government employees do not receive one penny as a rule if they quit their job before they finish the twenty or twenty-five years with their present employer, or if they are laid off before that time, no matter what the reason. A public school teacher in New Jersey, for instance, who takes a teaching job in New York State 10 miles away one term before reaching early retirement age in New Jersey forfeits all of his or her pension rights. Even the teacher who moves from a school in Glen Ridge, New Jersey, to one in Bloomfield, two blocks away, loses his pension credits. The same is true for a policeman in Oakland, California. In many governmental units (e.g., New York) to move even from one city department to another, say from the police department to public works, means a total loss of pension rights if done one day before the employee completes his or her twenty years "early retirement" service.

As a result, governmental employees—especially in local governments—are effectively tied to the job. The penalty for leaving before the twenty years early retirement date is exorbitant. Worse, employers—and especially other governments—are, with good reason, most reluctant to hire a teacher or a policeman with ten years of service elsewhere. They cost too much. They have to be paid their full pension when they retire; and yet they will not have served long enough to have made their full pension contribution. Under some pension plans, an employee hired at thirty-five and retiring at sixty-five will have cost a city or county around 20 percent more each year, because of "underfunding" of pension costs in his early years, than an employee in the same job paying the same salary and the same pension who started on the job in his early twenties.

Of all the "abuses" which the Pension Reform Act of 1974 aimed at correcting, none got a bigger play—deservedly—than the long vesting periods of some corporate pension plans and the resulting loss of pension rights of employees who quit or were laid off after many years of service and pension contributions. Now every private pension plan must "vest" after no more than ten years of service and pension contribution. Yet few pension plans of large corporations had as long a vesting period—the period before the quitting or laid-off employee has any pension to his credit—as the twenty or twenty-five years that are standard for governmental employees.

As long as governmental jobs could be assumed to have absolute job security, this could be defended as a minor cost of local self-government. Public-service unions resisted earlier vesting (even for teachers who, of all public-service employees, have the highest job mobility) as likely to interfere with their priority goals of more jobs, higher wages, higher pensions, and higher early retirement benefits. Now that lifetime job security for government employees can no longer be taken as an unalterable law of nature—especially after the cuts in New York City and California State employment—local government workers and their unions should, if they behave rationally, change their strategy. Early vesting would be for them the most intelligent trade-off against the demands for cuts in final pensions and in early retirement benefits with which they will be increasingly confronted.

But it might be more sensible not to trust to the chimera of "labor statesmanship," and to tackle this problem rather as one of individual liberty than City Hall politicking. It should be national policy to subject public-sector employers—that is, federal, state, and local governments—to the same ten-year rule for vesting that is now in force for private-sector employers and their pension plans.

In the long run, such a rule would actually ease the burden on governmental finances while at the same time improving the economic security of government employees. Governments would find it easier to lay off public-service employees as needed—i.e., teachers when the number of youngsters of school age drops sharply—while the laid-off employee with vested rights to pension payments upon reaching retirement age would find it much easier to get another job. Today the American governmental employee has a far higher pension than government employees in other countries* *if* he or she stays with the same employer till age sixty-five or at least for twenty or twenty-five years.

*Except perhaps in some cities of Japan. Tokyo, for example, as a result of "progressive" city government for the last ten years, is in even worse financial shape than New York City.

But he is also far worse off than government employees in any other major country (excepting again Japan, upon which the American Occupation unthinkingly imposed the American system), who can move freely among government employers anyway and carry their pension credits with them.

It is widely believed that local and state governments could save on pensions if only they did not yield to "exorbitant employee demands." This is nonsense. The pension funds of local and state governments (and of the federal government as well) will need *more* money; for years to come, pension fund requirements will be the first charge on local government and state government revenues. And this will be true even if the (surely exorbitant) early retirement benefits of government employees are cut back sharply despite union resistance. These governmental pension funds are so badly underfunded that they will require years of overfunding to get into balance.

The minimum of vesting needed to give governmental employees the pension fund protection and mobility equal to what ERISA now guarantees the employee of the business corporation will also cost more, a great deal more, than even the truly exorbitant early retirement deals of New York City in the late sixties and early seventies (or the yet more exorbitant ones of Tokyo's "progressive" mayor during the same period).

The real issue is not the cost of governmental pension plans collectively, but what they buy. And it is the wrong thing rather than too much. The present system can be called one of peonage through the pension fund; it is both antisocial and far too costly all around. The actions required to clean up these two pieces of unfinished pension fund business—the union-dominated funds and those of states, counties, and cities—is obvious. How soon they will be tackled depends on certain major political changes. First, Congress, business and labor unions, and above all the general public must accept that the pension plan— whether the employer be a private corporation, a government, or a non-governmental public-service institution such as the private university or hospital—has, within twenty-five years, become the major financial institution of America, and represents the major "asset" of most American families. It is a larger cost than health care, if not than education. It is crucial to economic security, job mobility, and individual freedom, in a society where nine out of ten working people are employees, and where eight out of ten can expect to live to age sixty and six out of ten to age seventy or beyond. The sound financing of pension fund obligations and policies, so as to safeguard pension fund assets, must become an unquestioned, first-priority goal of national policy, enforced on everyone—business, labor union, and governmental employer alike.

Finally, we have to realize that the change underlying the emergence of the pension funds is as important as the pension funds themselves. It is the sea change in population structure and demographics in the developed countries.

The Demographic Sea Change

The American pension fund is the most effective response so far to one of the most profound changes in the human condition: the survival of the majority of the population into old age and past their working years.

It is fashionable today to contrast our so-called callous disregard of the old with the loving care they supposedly received in the pre-industrial community and family. But this is arrant nonsense. The pre-industrial communities and their families did not have the problem at all; there were few survivors, even into what we would today call the prime of life, a man's fifties. The maximum life span, of course, remains virtually unchanged. There have been octogenarians and nonagenarians all through recorded history. But until the most recent days the man or woman who lived beyond forty was a "survivor" and the one who lived well beyond fifty a rare exception.

In the famous 1591 census of the Venetian trading port of Zara (a thriving city on the Adriatic), only people under fifty were counted as of working age. Those over fifty numbered only 365 out of a total population of 13,441, or about 1 in every 40.* Obviously, very few people were alive who were older than sixty or sixty-five. (Today in the United States, and in all other developed countries, people over sixty-five account for more than one-tenth of the population; those over fifty number one-quarter or more of the total population and two-fifths of the adult population.) Two hundred years after the Zara census, the population structure was still the same. Around 1800, Hamburg was probably (next to Amsterdam) the wealthiest and healthiest city of Europe, with strict control of immigration to keep out the poor and sick, and with the first city-wide public health system. Yet in the abundant and well-researched Hamburg records, people over fifty are conspicuous by their scarcity. The "patriarch" or "senior" of a patrician merchant family is a man in his early forties. Several decades later, in the mid-nineteenth century, Balzac still portrayed his *Femme de Trente Ans* as on the threshold of old age. And right through mid-Victorian days, every English

---

*Quoted in Fernand Braudel: *The Mediterranean* (New York: Harper & Row, 1972), Vol. I, p. 414.

census counted only people *under fifty* as part of the "working population." It seems there were almost no people above that age to be counted.

The very symbol of old age throughout history is the grandmother who looks after the small grandchildren, tells them fairy tales, dries their tears, and maybe even teaches them to read. Bent double with arthritis, having lost her teeth and able to eat gruel only, nearly blind with cataracts or glaucoma, she is in an advanced state of physical decay. Indeed, she is only available to look after the grandchildren because she is much too infirm to do other work. Yet this ancient crone can rarely have been much older in chronological age than forty-five or fifty, considering that for most women childbearing age began around fourteen or fifteen and ended before twenty-five.

The early "pension plans" for government employees—those of Austria and Sweden, for instance, which go back into the eighteenth century—did not provide a retirement pension at all. They were plans to take care of the surviving widow and young children of a deceased civil servant. Those few government employees who did survive to sixty or sixty-five could petition for a pension. But this was so rare that as late as 1900 the Emperor of Austria—with one of the world's biggest and, by the standards of 1900, most swollen bureaucracies—did not need even one full-time clerk to process the petitions for retirement pensions for the survivors.

A half century ago, when Japan organized its retirement system to take care of what was then considered a rapid increase in older people, average life expectancy was still below fifty and retirement was set at fifty-five. At that age the employee got two years of salary as a retirement bonus, which, according to life expectancies at the time, should have been ample to take care of the years he could still expect to be around.*

As to "loving care" for the old people in pre-industrial communities, the folk tales of every Western country portray nothing but contempt, ill treatment, and scorn for the surviving old. So did the works of the great Japanese painters of the eighteenth century such as Taiga, Hakuin, or Sengai, all three of whom had one favorite subject: biting portrayals of the wretchedness and loneliness of, and contempt for, the old in a country supposedly renowned for its reverence for age. The only reason why the beloved grandmother of folklore and childhood reminiscences had so much time for her grandchildren was that the adults of the family excluded her, relegating her to loneliness in the chimney corner. It was not that the children were allowed to eat with her; she had been banished from the table of the adults and was forced to eat with the children.

Three major factors together determine population structure: the birthrate, the infant mortality rate, and the life expectancy of those surviving infancy. Of these, life expectancies of the survivors of infancy was the first to improve significantly—largely as a result of the great improvements in public health and sanitation from the mid-nineteenth century on. The last of the three to change was infant mortality; significant improvement only began toward the very end of the nineteenth century, around 1895 or so. From then on, however, infant mortality rates in the West and in Japan fell sharply for thirty years, and then kept on declining slowly for another ten years until they stabilized at a very low level around the time of World War II.

The demographic change has thus been under way for

---

*Japan now has the same average survival expectation as the West for people reaching adulthood: age seventy-four or so for men and seventy-eight to eighty for women.

well over 100 years. But it only became a "demographic revolution," which made those older people surviving past working age into a dominant group, when the babies who did not die in the 1890s reached the arbitrary retirement age of sixty-five in the 1960s and early 1970s. In 1955, the change could already be predicted but it had not yet taken place; by 1975, it had become an accomplished fact.

In 1935, when Social Security came into force, there was alive one American over sixty-five for every nine or ten people in the labor force. Today the ratio is one to four. The number of Americans past age sixty-five has grown in the last forty years almost three times as fast as the labor force. Yet these forty years are the period of fastest labor-force growth in American if not in all Western history, primarily because the participation of married women in the labor force rose from almost nothing (except on the farm) to 50 percent.

The demographic sea change of the last seventy years has thus created, for the first time in human history, both a very large group of "middle-aged" people, that is, people past the age of family formation and child-rearing yet still fully capable of working, and a smaller but still very large group of people surviving (by and large in fair health) into "old age," that is, past "retirement." Together these two groups, for whom pensions are a major concern, form a near-majority of the adult population in all developed countries.

In these countries the number as well as the proportion of people older than traditional retirement age will still grow for at least a decade. In the United States, people over sixty-five numbered in 1975 around 22 million—a little less than 10 percent of the population. They will number 30 million by the mid-eighties—almost 12 percent of the total population, 20 percent of the adult population, and 30 percent of the labor force. And from then on, they will stay at around that percentage unless there is another "baby boom" comparable to that of the 1950s. In the other developed countries, including the Soviet Union, the demographic situation is roughly the same.

The two groups for whom retirement and retirement pensions are a major concern—the retired and the working people over fifty and approaching retirement age—will therefore increasingly form a "population center of gravity" in the developed countries and are likely increasingly to dominate the politics, moods, concerns, and economic and social policies of these countries.

During the late sixties and early seventies the Permanent Youth Revolution was widely proclaimed, for instance by such writers as Charles Reich of Yale in his best-selling book *The Greening of America.* But one could say even then with certainty that the Youth Revolution was only a ninety-days wonder. For when it was at its loudest and most visible, in the late sixties, we had already had a full decade of "baby bust." This decline began in 1960–61 with dramatic drops in the birthrate in the United States and all other developed countries, and, inevitably, a very sharp drop in the number of teenagers beginning in the mid-seventies. The Youth Revolution therefore had to be a transitory phenomenon. The permanent change, the real "revolution" during those years, was the emergence of a very large population of people over sixty-five as a new population center of gravity. And only a catastrophe on the scale of nuclear war or the massive pestilence of a new Black Death could for the foreseeable future undo this change.

In their fashion, their rhetoric, and the slogans of the mass media, the developed countries may continue to stress youth (though it is not very likely). But they are bound, increasingly, to become "middle-age-dominated" and "pension-focused" in their actions and concerns, whatever their rhetoric. The word "revolution" is tossed around carelessly whenever the hemline of women's skirts goes up or down an inch or the publisher of a third-grade speller brings out a new edition. But both the sea change in demographics and the emergence of pension fund socialism in America deserve to be called revolutions. Indeed, the demographic change may well be a more important event than those "revolutions" to which historians (especially Marxists and post-Marxists) are wont to pay exclusive attention: the "bourgeois" or "Communist" revolution, or even the "Industrial Revolution" in technology. Above all, they may have more direct and faster impact than any of these on individual and family.

So far only American society has even tackled the issues of this demographic revolution. The corporate pension fund can, of course, only indirectly help with the emotional, physical, and cultural problems of aging or with the stress which the survival of large numbers of old people puts on the family, although the contribution which an adequate income makes to individual dignity and to health should not be underrated. But within a few years—no more than ten—the pension funds will have built up enough assets and will cover enough employees to provide a fairly decent income, even by American standards, to something like two-thirds of all Americans reaching retirement age (provided only that inflation does not erode or destroy the accumulated savings). In every other country, whether Socialist, Communist, or capitalist, the great majority of the aged receive only a governmental pension, which almost everywhere is well below the level of U.S. Social Security, below any of our notions of "poverty threshold," and indeed for the great majority of recipients, in England, for example, barely at subsistence level.

The American pension fund also represents a bigger

shift in ownership than any that has occurred since the end of feudalism. In fact, one could argue that it represents a more radical shift in ownership than Soviet communism. It is not only, according to orthodox Marxist-Leninist theory, "ownership *by* the masses," which characterizes the "first stage of socialism," it is also "ownership *for* the masses"— the Marxist-Leninist slogan for the second and final stage of the "perfect Socialist society," which even Soviet Russia does not promise to reach for a long time.

The shift to an economy in which the "worker" and the "capitalist" are one and the same person, and in which "wage fund" and "capital fund" are both expressed in and through "labor income," is radical innovation and at odds with all received theory. That the "capital fund" is created out of labor income—and payments into a pension fund, whether made by employer, employee, or both, are "deferred wages" and "labor costs"—is perfectly sound Marxism. But it is totally incompatible with both classic economic theory and Keynesian neoclassicism. That this "capital fund" is in turn channeled back through "labor income"— which is what pension payments are—is again perfectly sound classical theory. But it is totally incompatible with Marxism, even at its most revisionist.* At the same time, ownership of the economy's productive resources by the employee pension funds maintains both the mobility of the employee and the mobility of capital, both individual freedom and the rational allocation of resources to productivity.

Twenty-five years ago, anyone who suggested a program for providing the bulk of America's employees with retirement incomes through corporate pension plans would have

---

*It is, if anything, a twentieth-century version of the "Philansteries" and of the utopias of the French "Romantic Socialists" of the early nineteenth century— Fourier, for instance, and in particular Saint-Simon, whom both classical economists and Marxists thought they had committed for good to the lunatic asylum of history.

been dismissed as a visionary, and his proposal as impossible, financially as well as economically. If he had then proposed that big business should voluntarily turn controlling ownership over to the employees, he would have been considered an extreme "radical," way out on the lunatic fringe, by left and right alike. All reasonable men would have agreed that such a change in ownership could come about only through a violent upheaval—a genuine, cataclysmic revolution.

What is utterly amazing, therefore, is that the actual accomplishment of these "impossible" and "radical" goals has gone practically unnoticed.

The Revolution No One Noticed

There is a vast literature on pension funds. But it deals either with actuarial matters, such as vesting and funding of pension claims for the individual, or with investment portfolios and investment performance. The Congress of the United States spent more than two years on ERISA, the Pension Reform Act of 1974, hearing countless witnesses, conducting dozens of studies, and considering a raft of alternative proposals. Yet there is not one mention in those thousands of printed pages of the social or political implications of the pension funds, and very little concern for the economic impacts, on capital market or capital formation, for example. The entire discussion is on actuarial and portfolio management matters only.*

*The only discussions of the economic and social implications of the pension funds appeared twenty-five and twenty years ago, well before the pension funds developed into major investors and owners, and well before their impacts could have been assessed. Altogether there have been only three such discussions: an article of mine—far too pessimistic—"The Mirage of Pensions" (discussing the union demands of the late forties), in *Harper's Magazine*, February 1950, before

Even more amazing is the fact that debate over the social and political structure of modern society, in this country as well as outside, pays not the slightest attention to the accomplished fact of the American pension fund and to its ownership of industry's share capital. Indeed, there are quite a few proposals around to invent the pension fund, as if it did not exist as yet; and the proposed inventions are vastly inferior to the existing reality.

In this country, for instance, one such proposal that is much praised is that of Louis Kelso for part-ownership of business through profit-sharing pension funds for its employees. Kelso proposes to make "capitalists" out of America's employees by rendering them "owners" in the business that employs them. This is, of course, the old "industrial democracy" plan all over again, though it is now called "people's capitalism." And the same objection still applies that led Charles Wilson to reject it twenty-six years ago; it would make the workers "owners" but, for half or more of them, in bankrupt companies or declining industries, thus depriving them of the pension they need.

Indeed, we know from long experience that Kelso's "industrial democracy" is not even a prescription for industrial peace. It almost guarantees industrial bitterness. To tie the employee's financial self-interest—in which support in his non-working old age is paramount—to the com-

---

the first of the modern pension plans was born; Adolph A. Berle's book—far too optimistic—*Power Without Property* (New York: Harcourt Brace, 1959); and Paul P. Harbrecht's study for the Twentieth Century Fund, *Pension Funds and Economic Power* (also 1959), which deals mainly with the problems of trusteeship. Of the three, Berle and I predicted major consequences for economic structure, capital markets, and so on, and we predicted basically things that have not happened, such as a decisive impact of the pension funds on industrial relations and "industrial democracy." Since 1959 nothing has been written, though in those sixteen years the assets of private pension funds have risen more than tenfold and their ownership stake in American business has gone up from less than 3 percent to more than 30 percent.

pany's fortunes through a profit-sharing pension fund invested in the employing company's stock works beautifully as long as the company's profit and stock price keep on going up. The first year, however, in which earnings drop and the stock price goes down, the happy "capitalist" employee-owner turns into a deeply disturbed and hostile critic. He feels he has been had—and he is right. He considers himself victimized; even if earnings and profits start going up again, he will not regain his confidence that his retirement pension is as secure as it should or could be. Yet the most prosperous business will have its bad years.

It is not so surprising that the old employee illusion of worker-ownership of "their" business financing their retirement pensions, is still around; old illusions die hard. What is amazing is that no one in the debate on the Kelso plan—neither advocates nor critics—shows any awareness of the existence of pension funds which accomplish the Kelso goal of making the American worker into a "capitalist" without the financial hazards and costs of the Kelso approach. Senator Russell Long (Democrat for Louisiana), one of Kelso's disciples, pushed through the Congress in the fall of 1975 a bill giving special tax privileges to pension plans which invest their monies exclusively in the company the workers work for. He ignored the massive evidence that the American worker, for sound investment reasons, much prefers the GM-type private pension fund that gives him what he needs, namely, financial security for his retirement years. He surely did not realize that his bill is essentially an incentive to expropriate workers' pension funds so as to finance weak companies that otherwise could not get capital. And he clearly was never told that there are already retirement plans in being for the majority of America's employees.

The American achievement is noticed just as little outside the United States. In Europe, Ota Šik—years ago the most brilliant of orthodox Stalinist theoreticians, later the economic architect of the "Prague Thaw" and Deputy Prime Minister of Czechoslovakia, and now in exile as a professor at the University of Basel—has proposed to establish "democratic socialism" by building a nation-wide, union-managed employee retirement fund out of corporate profits, which in turn would then invest in the country's businesses. In his original 1969 proposal, Šik wanted his plan to aim at eventually owning, after twenty-five years, about 10 percent of a country's businesses. This struck a great many European Socialists as being much too radical. Yet when Šik put forward his plan, the American pension funds already owned nearly twice as much (some 18 percent) of American business. Neither Šik nor his European critics, whether on the left or right, so much as mentioned the American reality.

Shortly thereafter the Danish Labor government, to placate its left wing, actually introduced a version of the Šik plan into its parliament. Under this proposal, the workers' pension fund—one for the entire country—would, by the year 2000, have obtained ownership of about 10 to 15 percent of Danish industry (at which time the employee pension funds of America will own at least 60 percent of American business). This was considered so radical, even by Danish liberals, that the proposal had to be withdrawn in a hurry.

In 1975, finally, leading members of Sweden's ruling Socialist Labor Party put forth a plan for the "attainment of socialism" and of "industrial democracy." The plan proposes to use 20 percent of the *post-tax* annual profits of every large Swedish company to buy shares of the company and put them into a nation-wide employee pension plan. By 1975, however, American companies already had put 30 percent of their *pre-tax* profits, or at least twice as much as the Swedes proposed, into pension plans primarily invested in equity. At the very fastest, with nothing but years of high profits for all companies, the Swedish plan would take until long past the year 2000 to give the pension funds of its employees the ownership share (30 percent) which American pension funds had already attained in 1975.

These Scandinavian versions of the Šik plan differ in important details from America's "pension fund socialism" —and for the worse. The one nation-wide pension fund they propose would have to hold shares in every Danish or Swedish company, and would neither be able to sell holdings nor to buy securities other than those it gets as an annual profit-equivalent. It would be frozen into its holdings—and so would be its pension beneficiaries. The fund thus could not get out of declining companies or declining industries; indeed, its very size and prominence would make such action politically impossible. The employees would therefore almost certainly get a far smaller pension in the end than they would get from a fund that has freedom to invest like the pluralist, autonomous, and decentralized funds of the American system.

Economically, this compulsory subsidy to the old and declining businesses is equally undesirable. It freezes the country's economy into today's pattern at a time of rapid economic and technological change. In fact, such a plan condemns Scandinavia to the fate Britain has inflicted on herself since World War II. Old businesses, no matter how obsolescent, would be amply fed with capital. But with the fund confined to investing in the existing profitable and large businesses, capital for new businesses and for the growth sectors of the economy would be virtually unobtainable in these countries. Also such an official, more or less governmental fund could only invest in its own country.

And exclusion of investment in the world economy is hardly the right action for a very small country today, whether in the interest of the future pensioners or of the country itself.

Even advocates of these plans admit their shortcomings and are bothered by them. "But," they ask, "how else could the job be done?" Clearly, they have never even heard of the American development. The opponents of these plans —including some of Scandinavia's most knowledgeable economists, bankers, and business leaders—are equally unaware of the American development and have no idea, apparently, that American pension fund socialism exists; that it already has gone much further toward "socialism" and "employee ownership" than the most radical of the European plans; and that it has done so with far more financial and economic flexibility and far less danger of trade union abuse of pension fund power and wealth. Even Ota Šik, who is much concerned lest his own plan degenerate into a trade union racket, does not appreciate the United States' accomplishment, let alone that in America employee pension funds built up out of business profits have already become the controlling owners of big business. Ironically, both Šik and the Scandinavians present their plans as "Europe's answer to capitalist America." And when someone tells them of the American development (as I did at a congress in Malmö, Sweden, several years back), no one believes it: "We would have heard of it if it were true."

Indeed, no one seems to have heard of it in the United States. The worker knows that there is a pension fund, and workers over forty-five or fifty years of age are vitally interested in it. But not one in a thousand seems to realize that through his pension plan he actually owns American business. Union leadership, similarly, knows that there is a pension plan and is much concerned with its provisions and its investment performance. Yet union leaders seem not to understand that the pension plan is actually the "employer" today.

The same is true of management. All of them know, of course, that the "institutional investors" are the major source of capital funds today. And all of them know that "institutional investor" is simply another term for "pension fund." All of them know that these "institutional investors" together own the controlling interest in their company and that, indeed, the company could not be financed unless the "institutional investors," or pension funds, were willing to invest in it. And since the debate about ERISA a few years ago, most managements have come to realize that contributions to the pension plan of their own company are a very large and steadily growing cost, amounting in most companies to at least one-third of the earnings of a good year, which, under ERISA, will go up to 50 percent of gross pre-tax profits for a good many companies within the next few years.

But almost no management I know has made the simple calculation which puts together the percentage of pre-tax profits that goes into their own company's pension fund and the percentage of post-tax profits that already belongs to the "institutional investors," that is, to other companies' pension funds. Few therefore realize that pension funds, their own and those of others, already get as much of the company's profits as the tax collector and more, far more, than anyone else.

Let us look at the 1973 figures for six companies in the chemical industry, ranging from a large one with sales of $1 billion to two fairly small ones with sales of $100 million a year each. The total combined profits, before pension fund contribution and taxes, equal 100. Pension fund contributions (which are, of course, tax-deductible) equal 20, leaving a pre-tax profit of 80, on which corporation income tax of a little over 40 percent was paid. Forty percent of 80 amounts to 32, which leaves a post-tax profit of 48, of which the institutional investors (practically all pension funds) were entitled to one-third or to 14 to 15 percentage points of the original 100. Pension funds, both the company's own (20) and other companies' funds (14 to 15), thus took 34 to 35 percent of profit before pension charges and taxes; the federal government took 32; other governments (especially state governments) took 5; leaving less than one-third for the "outside" investors.

These figures grossly understate the pension fund take. In the first place, 1973 was before ERISA sharply increased company contributions to the pension fund. Secondly, the chemical industry is, as a whole, not very labor-intensive. In a labor-intensive industry such as construction, let alone such service industries as retailing or health care, contributions to the company's pension fund tended even in 1973 to run as high as 40 percent of pre-tax profits. Third, these are figures for a good, indeed a record year, in chemical industry earnings; two years later, in 1975, when earnings were down for the chemical industry, the same six companies had to put 35 percent of their profits before pension charges and taxes into their own pension funds. Altogether, most companies must now count that even in a good year well over half of all total profits will belong to employees' pension funds, either as the company contribution to its own fund or as the share of the pension funds of employees from other companies. Even Uncle Sam, in other words, has become a junior partner. And for outside, independent, non-institutional investors, no more than a fifth or less of gross profit may be left, even in a prosperous year.

What this means for financial policy, capital structure, or

dividend policy, almost no management has apparently thought about much. Yet, as the next section of this book will discuss, the implications are startling.

In the debate over the structure of American economy and society, the pension funds are rarely even mentioned. One example are the figures regarding the "distribution of personal wealth" which have become popular, now that the traditional figures for the distribution of income no longer support attacks on America as a country of growing inequality and inequity. Yet these figures leave out entirely the claim to a retirement pension. This is not a "possession." It is not "property" in the traditional meaning of the term, in that it cannot be bought or sold, pledged or borrowed against. It is not even a specific amount until the individual reaches the point at which he begins to draw a pension; and even then the total is dependent on how long he survives.

But the claim to a pension is clearly "wealth." Indeed, it is likely to be the largest single asset for the middle-aged American family, exceeding in value the owner-occupied single-family home, as well as the automobile—the two traditional "most valuable possessions" of the American family. To exclude it makes any wealth figure meaningless and indeed phoney. If it were included—which could be done fairly easily on a probability basis—the "distribution of personal wealth" would show as high a degree of equality as that of income, and perhaps a higher one in that pension claims are distributed according to age as much as according to income.

Yet it does not seem to occur to anyone in today's discussions of the distribution of personal wealth—whether government statisticians, Socialist advocates like Michael Harrington in his widely read *Socialism,** or even those who criticize both the concept and the figures—that the pension

*(New York: Saturday Review Press, 1972).

fund assets have to be included before any figure on the distribution of wealth in the United States can be put together or properly analyzed.

The Corporation Income Tax

Another example of the general failure to perceive the pension funds and their meaning is the debate over the corporation income tax. With the emergence of pension funds as the controlling owners of American big business, the corporation income tax has become a punitive tax on the American worker and a subsidy to the "fat cats," the people with large incomes. For people already being taxed at a rate of 50 percent or more, that is, a married couple with net earnings of $100,000 a year or more, a corporation income tax of 48 percent means little additional tax burden. And for people earning a good deal more, say $250,-000 a year, a substantial portion of whose income comes from dividends, the corporation income tax may actually *lower* the total tax burden. But for the pensioner who receives all or most of his income from his corporate pension fund, the corporation income tax sharply raises the effective rate of tax on the income of which he is the beneficial owner and ultimate recipient. It may bring his actual tax burden to 50 percent or so. For that part of his income—and it may be 70 percent or so—which represents, in effect, corporate dividends on the holdings of the pension fund is taxed at 48 percent, with him paying another tax, amounting to 15 to 20 percent of the amount he actually receives, for a total that in many cases exceeds 50 percent and rarely falls much below that figure.

The corporation income tax has thus become a highly regressive tax, and one that is paid increasingly by the employees, especially those least able to afford a high rate of taxation—older retired workers. It is in effect a tax to "soak the poor." Yet any proposal to reduce the corporation income tax, or to allow the individual taxpayer to offset it in his tax return, is immediately shouted down as a "giveaway to the rich" by the labor unions, i.e. the representatives of the people who are most penalized. Actually, nothing would so effectively promote greater equality of income as to eliminate the corporation income tax, or at least that part of it which is levied on the holdings of the corporate pension funds. This would give the lowest income group in the adult population, the retired older people, substantially more purchasing power without inflationary impact.

The facts should be obvious, yet no one seems to notice them—neither the labor union leaders, the tax economists, nor even the businessmen who argue vociferously against the corporation income tax as a tax on capital formation and therefore on economic and job growth. All of them clearly assume that America's large corporations—which together account for three-quarters or so of the corporation income tax—are still owned individually by "rich men" rather than collectively, through the pension trusts, by the low- and middle-income earners, the employees of American business.

The demographic change—and it is fully as revolutionary—has gone equally unnoticed. The figures are known, of course; but no one seems to consider their impact.

Yet the demographic change makes traditional theories (classical, Marxian and Keynesian alike) and the economic policies based on them obsolete. It raises up a "welfare society" totally different from the one liberals advocate and conservatives deplore. Indeed, one incompatible with what either considers the "Good Society." And it changes the traditional meaning of key concepts such as savings, investment, and full employment, on which policies for economy and society have been based, whether liberal or conservative, traditional or radical.

The demographic change creates new major problems of productivity and capital formation. It makes the economy permanently inflation-prone and makes "undersaving" rather than the Keynesian "oversaving" the endemic threat to economic stability.

The demographic change in the developed countries, and particularly in the U.S., has meaning far beyond these countries themselves. It adds a "generational gap" between the world's developed industrialized countries and the underdeveloped Third World to the tension between "rich" and "poor" and "white and "non-white."

This book deals with accomplished facts, which, however, popular perception does not yet apprehend and with which our policies do not yet deal: facts of America's accomplished pension fund socialism, and of the demographic changes that underlie it.

2. Pension Fund Socialism: The Problems of Success

The Dangers of Success

The pension funds have become America's new "tycoons" —surely the most unlikely masters any society ever had. They have attained this position without any struggle, any crisis, any major "problems." It is an amazing success story —all the more amazing in that no one apparently has paid much attention to it.

But success always creates its own problems. Increasingly, the problems of pension fund socialism will become central issues in American society, economy, and politics. And because the rise of pension fund socialism—and the demographic changes that underlie it—have attracted so little attention, we are unprepared for these problems. This, rather than the problems themselves, probably represents the greatest threat. There are problems arising out of the very commitment to organized support of older people through a pension system. There are fundamental problems of economic structure, economic policy, and economic theory. And there are problems of authority, legitimacy, and control—that is, basically political (though mainly non-governmental) problems.

Finally, the rise and success of the pension funds puts into question the entire role and future of Social Security, and may lead to far more drastic Social Security reform than anything envisaged so far.* For the majority of American employees—those enrolled in the pension plan of an employer or in a self-employed pension plan—Social Security is rapidly becoming a supplementary rather than a primary source of retirement income. Its costs are high and rising, and the benefits go increasingly to people other than the ones who pay for Social Security—that is, to people without an employer or self-employed pension plan—if not as "welfare" payments to people who themselves have made no Social Security payments. At the same time, the Social Security system is in serious financial trouble, and indeed is technically insolvent.

Population Dynamics, Birthrates, and Dependency Ratios

The worker who has part of his paycheck put into a pension account foregoes immediate consumption; someone else, already on a pension, consumes instead. In exchange, the worker receives a claim to consumption in the future. But this claim can be satisfied only out of the production of the future. The shoes, automobiles, loaves of bread, and medical treatments today's worker will want to buy with his pension check twenty-five years hence are not being produced today and stored away. They will have to be provided out of the production of twenty-five years hence, and

*For example, by Martin Feldstein in his remarkable article, "Toward a Reform of Social Security," in *The Public Interest*, Summer 1975.

at the expense of the consumption of someone else actually producing goods and services twenty-five years hence.

Pension fund socialism creates individual independence. The older people are no longer dependent on charity or on the goodwill and economic success of their children. They have a *claim*, not just a *need*. We ought to remember this before we complain how "unfeelingly" our society is treating them. But as a group, the retired people are just as "dependent" as before on the capacity of the people at work to produce a surplus of goods and services for them, and on the willingness of the "productive population" to hand the surplus over against the claims of the retired people.

Those few economists who pay attention to population and demographics point out that the ratio between "productive population" and "dependent population" in the United States is not deteriorating and may actually improve. For the number of small children has been going down faster than the number of old people past working age—sixty-five—has been increasing.

However, this is irrelevant. The worker who takes $20 out of his own pay envelope to buy shoes for his child does not look upon this as a "transfer payment." He is not supporting a stranger. As long as the money stays in the family, he does not see himself as cutting down on his own consumption to support a "dependent." The same $20 taken out of his paycheck to be put into a pension fund or into Social Security is, however, a cut in his income and in his purchasing power. In other words, what matters socially and politically is not the ratio of "productive" to "dependent" population, but the ratio of productive members of the working population to the no-longer productive— retired—adults.

The American birthrate dropped between 1960 and

1965 by more than 25 percent and it has not yet turned up. With twenty as the age at which significant numbers of young people in today's America first become available for "real" jobs, the number of new entrants into the work force will begin to decrease sharply by the end of the seventies and will keep on going down at least until the late 1980s. Whatever happens to the birthrate in the interim period can have impact only after 1995.

From the mid-sixties until the mid-seventies, America each year had to find some 40 to 50 percent *more* jobs for young entrants into the working population than in any year between 1950 and 1965—the result of the "baby boom" between 1948 and 1959. From 1978 on, we will have each year up to 30 percent *fewer* entrants into the working population than we had in the ten years from 1967 to 1977.

The age at which people enter the work force may no longer go up. After a century of steady rise—from twelve or so in 1850 for the great majority, especially youngsters on the farms, to fifteen in 1935 when Social Security first was enacted, to twenty or later nowadays when half of the young people attend school beyond high school—the age of entrance into the working population has probably stabilized at around twenty to twenty-two for the majority, with a significant minority keeping on in professional or technical education and thus staying out of the labor force several more years. It is unlikely that there will a significant reversal toward earlier entrance into the labor force. If we make it possible for people under twenty to gain some work experience—and this is clearly highly desirable—it would be as "apprentices," "trainees," or "interns" rather than as full-time workers expected to do an adult's job and getting an adult's pay. We cannot expect, in other words, that enough young people will start work earlier than the current age of twenty to twenty-two to offset to any extent the sharp drop in the total number of young people reaching adolescence and adulthood.

We also can no longer expect the proportion of working wives in the labor force to increase significantly. With four to five out of every ten married women already at work, mostly full-time, we probably have reached the saturation point. At the very least, the steep increase in work-force participation on the part of women is bound to flatten out. Women in the labor force may get better jobs and greater opportunities, especially if economic conditions are propitious. But their total number or proportion is unlikely to increase much. Indeed, the proportion of married women who work may well go down somewhat in the next ten years. Many demographers expect birthrates to rise, though only moderately. For the last few years, since 1972 or so, the birthrate has been just below the "net reproduction rate" at which birthrates balance death rates. At the same time, the U.S. population today contains a singularly high proportion of young women of childbearing age—the result of the ten years of "baby boom" after 1948. There is some evidence that many, if not most, of these young women have only postponed their pregnancies and fully intend to have at least two children during their fertile years.* This would mean that fewer young married women would be available for work, at least full-time work, until their children are in school or in their teens. Any such rise in the birthrate would therefore mean a further deterioration in the dependency ratio—that is, in the demands for the support of non-producing people, the children and the old, on the income of the employed population.

The work-force situation and with it the dependency ra-

*See the paper, "The American Birth Rate: Evidences of a Coming Rise," by June Sklar and Beth Berkov, in *Science*, Vol. 189, No. 4204, August 29, 1975.

tio between people at work and retired older people will not be affected at all by the one group of births in which birthrates and birth numbers did not go down in the sixties, and only started to inch down in the seventies: black children born out of wedlock. The birthrates for the great majority of black families, married middle-class and working-class people, while still higher than for whites, have been falling steadily. But those for the poorest blacks—the "welfare mothers"—have been going up, with the biggest rise in the number of illegitimate babies born to very young black mothers aged fourteen to nineteen.

This is largely, one has to conclude, the result of welfare policies that were well meant but turned into cruelty. High welfare benefits first lured a large number of the least competent and most wretched into the most treacherous, demanding, and dangerous environment imaginable: the big city. When there was nothing in the city that these poor, untrained, and frightened people could do, we paid them for having children. The social consequences of this will be with us for a long time. And the trauma and agony will only be heightened in "good times" of overall labor shortage. The black illegitimate "welfare baby" of the 1960s and early 1970s will be a black teenager living on welfare in the early 1980s. No matter how badly he needs a job, there will be none for him, for our society—rightly or wrongly (I think wrongly)—does not believe that teenagers can or should have "real" jobs. They should be in school. Teenagers are essentially "unemployable." That this is not a matter primarily of attitude, skill or color is shown by the fact that five to seven years later the great majority of the same "unemployable" young blacks—at least the males—do have jobs, though rarely good ones. But until they are in their early twenties they are not considered to be part of the work force by society or by employers. But the majority of the "welfare babies" drop out of school in their early or mid-teens. Not having been taught anything much in school the first six or eight years, they quite rationally decide that they will not be taught much if they sit through another six years.

The rise in illegitimate black births, especially among very young black mothers, will therefore confront America and America's conscience with a horrible problem in a few years time. Yet the labor supply will be little affected by the problem—no matter how low the unemployment rates will be for other members of the work force (including black adults) or how high they will be for black teenagers.

In sum, the 1976 population available for work—the "full-employment labor force"—amounted to 93 million men and women, including people available only for part-time work, students for instance, or many married women with small children at home. With an 7 to 8 percent unemployment rate, this meant that 87 million people actually had jobs. By 1985, the total "full-employment labor force" (again including millions of people available only for part-time work) will have gone up to 100 millions or so. If unemployment drops to the "full employment rate" of 4 percent—a rate at which there is actually an acute shortage of people available for full-time work (especially adult males) and heavy inflationary pressure on wage rates*—the employed work force would come to 95 million.† Even if there is "full employment" in 1985, there will only be some 8 million more people at work than there were in the unemployment year of 1976.

But within the same ten years the number of Americans

---

*And a rate, incidentally, which in European unemployment statistics with their completely different definition of "unemployment" would be reported as less than 1 percent.

†This, by the way, is also the figure used by the U.S. Department of Labor, by the economists of the major unions, and by President Ford in his 1975 Labor Day speech as the number of people for whom the country has to find jobs in 1985 if there is to be "full employment."

aged sixty-five and over will go up by 8 millions, from 22 to 30 million people. For every three people surviving beyond age sixty-five, there is moreover one "surviving dependent"—usually a widow aged fifty-five or older, but still below the normal Social Security age of sixty-five—who as a rule has no income of her own, is too old and far too little skilled to find a job except in extreme labor-shortage periods such as a war economy, and is entitled to a "survivor pension" under Social Security and many private pension plans. In 1975 there were about 8 million recipients of such "survivor pensions," so that total Social Security recipients numbered 30 million—22 million people over sixty-five and 8 million "survivors." If the number of "survivors" grows in proportion to that of people older than sixty-five —and there is no reason to believe that this ratio will change much—we will have to take care of almost 40 million people who are "dependent" because they are past working age under our present definition of the proper age for retirement. In 1975, every three people at work had to support one old person in retirement or "surviving." This "dependency ratio"* is likely to shift to two and a half to one within ten years, even with full employment.

To be sure, the income needs of the retired, older people tend to be lower. The children are grown up and gone, the house is fully paid, and a good deal of their income—e.g., Social Security payments—is tax-free. They do, however, require more health care. Altogether an income level of 60 percent of the family's main breadwinner's income while working is acceptable—though hardly better—for the support of a retired couple. It is what three-fifths or two-thirds of all American employees—those who have pension plans in addition to Social Security—can expect to receive by the

*From now on, the term "dependency ratio" will be used to mean the ratio between total labor force and total of retired people and "survivors."

early or mid-eighties (subject, of course, to inflation). This means that today each employed American has to contribute almost one-fifth of his income to support the old and retired, and the "survivors," i.e., middle-aged widows of men who died before reaching retirement age, which is indeed what his combined Social Security and pension fund payments roughly amount to. Within ten years, however, this is likely to rise, even in full-employment periods, to one-quarter of his income or 25 cents out of every dollar earned.

The ratio may well be even worse. For increasingly "early retirement" is being built into both labor contracts and Social Security rules. This is, of course, a direct result of the emergence of private pension plans which provide an independent income. To reward employees for retiring early, as the retirement plans of local governments tend to do, is folly; and as an alternative to vesting pension rights in governmental pensions, it is vicious. But early retirement provisions that enable aging people to choose between working longer and receiving lower retirement pay at an earlier age are highly desirable. They represent a substantial increase in human freedom.

Even if used wisely, early retirement rights increase the number of people who no longer work and who are being supported out of the product of those who do—precisely at a time when the ratio between productive and dependent people in the American economy is already burdensome. The tension between the support needs of the retired population and the cash needs of the employed members of the labor force is therefore certain to increase. Yet no one seems to worry about the dependency ratio. Instead, it has almost become an axiom of American politicians, economists, and labor leaders that employees do not object to increases in Social Security and pension costs.

This is pure myth. Rising deductions for Social Security and pensions create conflicts within the labor force, between the older and the younger workers, and between the people at work and the older retired population.

Older workers have an interest in pensions and at the same time need less cash income than younger workers. In any wage settlement, the older workers therefore press for the largest increase in pension benefits rather than in wages. Younger workers under forty or forty-five, on the other hand, do not really think much about their retirement as yet—it is too far away. But, above all, it is the younger age group that has the greatest need for cash income. These are the years of cash pressures for children and their shoes; for housing; for furniture, appliances, recreation, and so on. Yet, it is precisely in these early years that the provision for retirement income should be at its peak. A dollar invested at age twenty-nine at 6 percent will be worth $8 at age sixty-five, whereas the same dollar invested at age fifty-three will be worth only $2 at age sixty-five. The cheapest way to finance old age pensions would surely be to put the burden on people under forty-five. After forty-five, and especially after fifty, putting money aside for retirement produces only insignificant retirement income. The marginal utility of money set aside in the last ten years before retirement is very small, probably a good deal smaller than the value of the satisfaction the payer might obtain by spending the same amount. The marginal utility of a dollar invested early in retirement is exceedingly high. But its "opportunity cost" is even higher.

The American worker, white-collar as well as blue-collar, has reacted to this dilemma in a perfectly rational way, but one that threatens to cripple the economy and, above all, the pension system. True, workers have no resistance to increasing retirement pensions—on condition only that their cash wages go up at least fast enough to compensate for the increased contributions to Social Security and pension funds. Take-home pay in the American mass production industries, it is often pointed out, did not increase faster than productivity until the late sixties, so that it had no inflationary impact until then. But in the early sixties total wage costs began to increase very much faster than productivity. One reason for this was the spiraling of health care costs; just as important was the steady increase in Social Security costs and especially private pension costs, which began around 1960. Whether the employee pays these or whether they are being paid for him by the employer is irrelevant. Either way they are "wage costs."

In the early seventies this pattern then accelerated again as a result of the very large number of young people, the products of the "baby boom" of the forties and fifties, entering the labor market. As young people have to do, they put their immediate needs well ahead of any concern for the future. But at the same time the number of people entering retirement age also increased sharply, thus creating a demand for a substantial expansion of Social Security and pension provisions.

The best (or worst) illustration of the effects of this built-in tension within the labor force are the pension plans of New York City, responsible in such large measure for the City's financial distress. It is easy to criticize Mayor Lindsay for having made such exorbitant settlements with the unions of City employees. But the mayor, as well as the leaders of the unions, was caught between the older members who wanted substantial pensions and the younger employees who wanted and needed maximum cash income. The outcome, given the political realities, was predictable: settlements which raised the wages for the working employees beyond the City's capacity to pay, and pension plans which did the same. The result was an explosion of New York City labor costs within a few short years, and inflationary pressures throughout the entire economy.

There is therefore a sense of continuing tension between younger and older workers, which can be assuaged by inflationary increases in both cash wages and contributions to pension plans, but cannot be eliminated as long as pension costs keep going up. Equally, there is a built-in tension between the people at work and earning, and the needs of the retired ex-workers on pension.

As a general policy, of course, everyone is in favor of generous retirement pensions; but in terms of specifics almost every employed worker regardless of age opposes paying out more of his or her income to support the aged and retired. If his income goes up, that is, if he has to increase his taxes or his contribution to Social Security and to the pension funds which pay the retirement bills, he expects at least a compensatory increase in his cash wages to "stay even." And the result is again both inflationary pressure and rising tensions between the various social groups.

These tensions between younger and older workers and between employed and retired people cannot be eliminated. They are the result of demographics and the price for the achievement of mass longevity. But they need not be aggravated by the pension system as they are being aggravated today. In fact, they can be made a great deal more bearable.

The American pension system still reflects the realities of fifty years ago when the idea of Social Security was first conceived in the mid-twenties, and of forty years ago when Social Security was actually born in 1935.

In the mid-twenties when Social Security was first proposed, the life expectancy at birth for white males—the country's main "breadwinners"—was fifty-five years; in early adulthood (after eliminating the white male children who had died earlier), it was fifty-eight; and at age sixty-five another three years, or age sixty-eight. By 1935, when Social Security was enacted, the figures were respectively fifty-nine, sixty-two, and seventy; in 1975, they stood at sixty-nine, seventy-four, and eighty, respectively. For white women reaching age sixty-five, the life expectancy has gone up from sixty-nine or seventy fifty years ago to eighty-four in 1975. For the young adult black, life expectancy is still below that of the white—age sixty-eight for black males at twenty-five. But life expectancies for those blacks, male or female, who reach age sixty-five are the same as those for whites; and the longer blacks survive thereafter, the higher (compared to whites) is their remaining life expectancy.

In the mid-twenties, a retirement age of sixty-five was ten years more than the blue-collar worker entering the labor force could expect to attain. Today it is fifteen years less.

When Social Security was enacted, in the mid-thirties, the country was in the depth of the Great Depression. The first aim of Social Security was therefore not, as had originally been planned, to take care of older people. Rather, it was to reduce the labor surplus and open up jobs for younger people who had to support a wife and children. Social Security highly penalized anyone who did not stop working completely at age sixty-five, regardless of his health or his own desires. The private pension plans then unthinkingly copied both the age limit and the compulsory retirement of Social Security.

But age sixty-five today corresponds to yesterday's age fifty-three or middle age, both because life expectancy and health have been improving and because the available jobs require increasingly less physical strength and impose increasingly less physical strain than the jobs of forty or fifty years ago. One cannot hoe the cotton patch if one needs a cane to walk, but one can easily be a telephone operator, a sales analyst, an engineer in the State Highway Department, or even a truck driver. And what is necessary today is to lighten the burden of supporting a rapidly growing population of older people on the more slowly growing "productive" work force.

Yet the only major exception we have so far permitted to the complete rigidity of our system is "early retirement." We need just as badly, for humanitarian reasons as well as economic ones, a policy of "late retirement"—one which enables people to retire early if they so desire, but which also allows them the option to continue working. Mandatory retirement before a worker reaches the age of average death expectancy (seventy-two or so) is hard to defend and, in effect, an anachronism. However, Social Security does not allow a retired male to earn any income except a few pennies till he is seventy-two, on pain of losing all or most of the Social Security benefits which, supposedly, he has fully paid for—and in addition he still must pay full Social Security tax on whatever he earns. Private pension plans do not penalize a man or woman for earning something, providing it is not with the employer out of whose pension plan he or she is being paid. But they offer even less of an incentive to keep on working than Social Security where, within the last few years, the law has been amended to give a person who keeps on working without drawing his Social Security benefits a slight, very slight, improvement in future benefits. The governmental plans, especially those of the cities, excessively reward employees for retiring early and as a rule do not even contain much incentive for working to age sixty-five.

What we need is a deliberate policy to encourage people to keep on working without penalty, with a sufficient incen-

tive (i.e., materially increased future income) and with guaranteed lump-sum payments to their heirs should they die
before they have drawn their pensions for a given number
of years (called "guaranteed death benefits"). At the very
least, people who keep on working and earning and who
thereby sacrifice Social Security benefits for which they
have paid in full, should not also have to continue to pay
Social Security taxes for which they will never get a return.
This would present neither actuarial nor insurmountable
financial problems. The country's largest industry-wide
pension fund, Teachers Insurance and Annuity Association
(TIAA)—mentioned earlier—has, for instance, an "early
retirement option" beginning at age sixty; but it has *no*
mandatory retirement age at which members have to retire
and start drawing their pension benefits. And by postpon-
ing the beginning of pension payments, the subscriber increases the size of the eventual pension. Yet TIAA pensions
cost no more than those of most corporate plans.

Even the pension program set up by Congress for the
self-employed (the Keogh Funds) allows—in sharp contrast
to the rules for Social Security and for most private pension
plans—the participant to delay drawing his pension until
he is seventy and a half years of age, and does not penalize
him for whatever he may earn while drawing his annuity.

There are good reasons for demanding that people at the
head of large organizations—be it a business, labor union,
army, university, or government—step down at a mandatory age. A decline in their physical or mental powers, or
even in their capacity to respond to change, can have disas-
trous consequences. And incipient senility is the one disease of which the victim himself remains unaware until it is
far advanced. Yet if he is the "boss," no one can force out
the aging man at the top. Only mandatory retirement can
do that. There is also good cause to insist on impartial and

frequent medical checkups to make sure that people in positions where physical or mental decline endangers others are still up to the job. Even if the top man is forced out by mandatory retirement age there is no reason to forbid, or to penalize, his doing other work, perhaps going back into private law practice, working as a consultant, starting his own small business, or running the chamber of commerce. The same applies for people no longer capable of holding a job requiring high standards of physical fitness or judgment. To the extent to which we enable people to keep working past a mandatory age—and certainly past the present age of sixty-five—without having to forfeit pension rights they have paid for, we will lessen the upward pressure on retirement pensions and with it the burden on the younger, working-age population.

We should make it possible for people who have chosen early retirement to come back into the labor force, and especially back to their former employer, particularly in labor-shortage years. Their pension payments should perhaps be suspended or cut back; but their pension rights should be fully maintained. A great many people think they want to retire early. But a great many also find out after a short time that they really only wanted a long vacation and would love nothing better than to go back to work again—not primarily for the sake of the income but for psychological satisfaction, companionship, and stimulation.

Today, with high unemployment and the last cohorts of the "baby boom" just entering the labor force, all this may sound pure fantasy. The time to do these things, however, will come soon enough in the early eighties, when job pressure from the new entrants into the labor force is certain to abate sharply (excepting only in the case of a major economic depression) while at the same time resistance against increasing pension contributions is bound to go up equally sharply among the younger employees. And if the labor unions, which are still much caught up in the verities of the 1930s, oppose such changes, they may soon find that the alternative is actually even less to their liking. It is a steadily spreading "Japanese system" in which people take their pensions and then go to work at much lower wages elsewhere, thus undercutting the entire union rate system. This is already happening in the construction industry. The "non-union" workers all over the country who are taking away construction jobs from union labor are not "outsiders"; they are, in large numbers, retired union members who draw benefits from a private pension plan and then go to work for less money for a non-union contractor.

But we also need to tackle the conflict between the younger workers' need for cash to spend and the advantage to them of paying into the retirement fund while they are still young. Such conflict makes for high pension costs as these younger workers try to postpone their pension contributions until middle age, when of course their pension dollar buys much less by way of retirement income. It also contributes heavily to the tension between older and younger employees, and thus creates constant inflationary pressure.

Now that employee pension rights are vested after ten years of service, it should be possible to provide an anticipatory credit that would enable the younger employee to pay in substantial amounts into his retirement fund through a form of installment loan, which he would then repay out of the retirement premiums of his later years. The risk of survival could be handled by means of the group life insurance, which most employees under pension plans carry anyhow. The devising and building of such a plan into the pension mechanism is one of the innovations most needed in finance—and the pension funds themselves could probably do it, given a little ingenuity and hard work.

The success of a plan which gears pension payments to the family life cycle can almost be guaranteed. The young employee usually knows that it is in his interest to pay in the maximum amount early; compound interest is not that difficult to grasp. Indeed, whenever employees have been given such an opportunity they have readily availed themselves of it with only a very slight incentive. Employees of non-governmental, non-profit institutions (e.g., a private university or a community hospital) can defer taxes on part of their income by putting additional money into their pension account under the tax-code provisions known as "Option III" and "Option IV." The rules are so complicated that even tax accountants do not always understand them; but the options are being used, and by a very large number of people. They are particularly popular among the younger college teachers, aged between thirty-five and forty-five, yet these people's salaries still tend to be fairly low, cash demands on them as great as on all young families, and the tax savings in their income bracket very modest indeed.

Even if we adjust the mandatory retirement age to current life and health expectancies, make the retirement plan more flexible, and encourage the worker to increase his retirement contribution when it buys the most, in the earlier years, we will not eliminate the fundamental demographic problem. To achieve longer life for larger numbers means a high dependency ratio, and a high support burden for those at work. But the ratio of one pensioner to two and a half working people is unnecessarily high and the result of thoughtless rigidity. The present policy, which assigns large numbers of healthy people to the scrap heap whether they want to "retire" or not, and at an age that still reflects the life and health expectancies of half a century ago, is also thoughtless cruelty. We could at least prevent the dependency ratio from going beyond one to three—and might be able to move it back to one to four.

This would enable us to increase the income of many older people, both those who actually retire and those who continue to work full-time or part-time. This would stop the imminent rise in the retirement burden on the people of working age to 25 percent of their income, and might actually lower it (maybe from the present 19 to 20 percent of an employed worker's income to 15 percent). At the same time we might significantly increase the productivity of the retirement dollar. The economic benefits from such changes would be very great. But the greatest benefits would be increased independence and increased dignity for older people and a decrease in social tension all around.

However, there are also serious tensions *within* the older, retired population. It may seem strange in this figure-happy country that no one really knows how many people are covered by pension plans other than Social Security, and how much by way of a pension they are likely to receive when they retire; further, it may strike us as odd that to translate such figures as are available for individuals into family or household income—the only meaningful terms—remains beyond anyone's knowledge or competence. But it is reasonably certain (barring only continuing sharp inflation) that from the early eighties on, when the private pension plans will begin to approach maturity, about one-half of all working people reaching retirement age can expect a family income of some 60 percent or more of the main breadwinner's pre-retirement income, composed of both retirement pay from a private pension plan and Social Security, with the private pension accounting for half or more of the total. This is a modest but barely adequate income. To this group might be added a smaller one (at most another fifth) of people with enough retirement pay from a pension fund to "sweeten" their Social Security and to bring their retirement income up to around 45 to 50 percent of pre-retirement earnings.*

These two groups—amounting together to between two-thirds and three-quarters of former working people reaching retirement age—will be relatively well off, at least as long as the main recipient (almost always the husband) of both Social Security and private pension stays alive. Barring serious inflation they should be able to manage, though rarely with much to spare or to lay aside.

The next group—one-fifth to one-quarter of the labor-force members reaching retirement age—will have only Social Security. If they get any retirement income from other sources, it will be too little to make a difference. They will therefore have not much more than bare subsistence income, if that much. Many of these people will have had poorly paying jobs and intermittent employment; their Social Security benefits will therefore be low to begin with. They will, for instance, find the additional premium for physicians' bills under Medicare a real burden.

And then there will be a fairly small fourth group—fewer than one-tenth of the people reaching retirement age—who will have no retirement benefits at all. Those relatively few among them who will have been on welfare in a big city all or most of their lives will (under today's rules) be taken care of fairly well. The others, however—the chronically sick or severely handicapped; the people who worked for themselves as farmers, craftsmen, or small shopkeepers without building up a self-employed pension plan or ade-

---

*These figures take into account that Social Security payments are tax-free in their entirety and private pension payments tax-free, at least in part, so that retirement earnings have to be compared with pre-retirement earnings after taxes and after Social Security deductions. Most of the published figures on the incomes of old people do not adjust for their different tax status.

quate savings, or single women who took care of an old parent and therefore never earned wages themselves—will get nothing or next to nothing. They will, in effect, be as destitute as were most of yesterday's old people. This fourth group poses a problem of "social welfare" which no pension system can handle, and which, in turn, no pension system should be expected to handle. Many of these people are also sick, emotionally disturbed, lonely, and in despair. But they can at least be economically supported by a wealthy and productive society, though only as "welfare clients" rather than "pensioners."

It is the third group—consisting of those people who had poor jobs during their working lives and now have only fairly low Social Security benefits—which poses the real problem. They represent the "proletariat" of the old age population, and no "pension reform," no incentive to postpone retirement, no funding and vesting can help them much, if at all. They were, after all, "marginal" as workers, which is why they are "marginal" as pensioners.

At the other end are the "rich" of the old age population, who receive both the highest Social Security benefits *and* the highest private pensions. The fact that these "rich" will constitute a majority of the people who reach retirement age—and also, because of their superior knowledge, skill, and social mobility, will have the best chances to have saved and to be able to continue to earn on the side—can only worsen the tension between the groups. The "rich" must feel that they have earned their position; they certainly paid for it. Most of them will be "rich" only in comparison with the "old age proletariat," of course; their absolute income standard will be modest, well below the standard they lived on while working. Yet they will actually subsidize the "proletariat." For under Social Security, low-wage earners receive back a good deal more than they paid in, whereas high-wage earners receive back a good deal less.

But the "proletarians" will only see that they receive less, far less, than the "rich," and far less than an adequate income. They will be conscious of a gross inequality of income distribution in old age society in America. The fact that this group of "old age proletarians" will contain a disproportionate number of minorities—above all, surviving widows, though also a relatively large number of racial-minority members, blacks as well as Puerto Ricans and Spanish-Americans—will hardly help.

This is a problem of money. But it is a problem of justice rather than economics, a problem where "right" is up against "right," which means that it cannot be tackled within the pension system, whether private or Social Security. The relatively small sum needed to bring old age income for the "old age proletarians"—the former "working poor"—up to a minimum standard (say the "poverty level" for a family of two) will have to come out of general tax revenues and be paid as "welfare" rather than as insurance or pension. This is one problem the so-called negative income tax could solve, or at least assuage, at a manageable cost.

The Economic Problems of Pension Fund Socialism

Way back in the twenties, before the Keynesian tide engulfed economics, a college course particularly popular in Europe was entitled "The Problems of Socialism." Central among the "economic problems of socialism" was concern with capital formation and capital allocation under a "market socialism."* These long-forgotten concerns are surfac-

*The most distinguished thinker and writer of this tradition was the Polish economist Oscar Lange, who, after the Nazi invasion of Poland, taught for many

ing again today. They are indeed going to become central questions for a society which, like the United States, has "socialized" the means of production without "nationalizing" them.

When General Motors, around 1950, set off the pension fund avalanche, the New York Stock Exchange had just proclaimed a program called "Peoples' Capitalism" to make the great majority of American wage earners "capitalists" and owners of common stock through the Wall Street mechanism. This was always unlikely to work. Any mass market, such as the one which the New York Stock Exchange envisaged for securities, needs merchants: informed buyers for the customers. It needs intermediaries —and the Stock Exchange's hope that the mass market consumer would buy directly from the "producer," through the Stock Exchange, was therefore naïve to begin with. But it did not seem impossible in 1950.

Today, twenty-five years later, "Peoples' Capitalism" has turned into "Pension Fund Socialism." A far larger number of Americans are "owners"—or rather, legally, "beneficial owners"—of common stock than the Stock Exchange ever hoped for. But the capital market is not Wall Street. The capital market of the United States is now the pension funds. Wall Street has been overtaken by "structural obsolescence," which has turned it into a depressed industry.

The Stock Exchange's "Peoples' Capitalism" envisaged millions of individual decision makers in the capital market: the individual buyers and sellers of common shares. But today's American capital market is dominated by no more than 1,000 to 1,500 large corporate pension funds. In the U.S. these tend to be both "benefits managers" concerned

---

years at the University of Chicago before returning to Poland to die, unmolested by his Communist masters, but silenced by them.

with pension administration and "financial managers" responsible for investments. (Elsewhere these two roles tend to be quite strictly separated.) But even in the U.S. the day-to-day investment decisions are usually delegated to an even smaller group—a few hundred teams of "asset managers": economists, financial analysts, and portfolio managers, heavily concentrated in turn in the largest banks and insurance companies.

The cry of "excessive concentration of economic power" is a conditioned reflex to any structural change in the American economy. It is already being heard on Wall Street about the new capital market structure, and will surely soon be picked up in the press, in the Congress, and by assorted "populists"—whether consumerists or government regulators. But it can be dismissed as pure red herring. The decision makers in the U.S. capital market still greatly outnumber those of any other developed country. Germany's capital market, for instance, functions quite well with three decision makers: the three large banks, which account for four-fifths or more of all German capital market transactions. In Japan the number—again mostly the large, so-called city banks—is not much higher.

Above all, the U.S. capital market of the "asset managers" lacks and will continue to lack the one characteristic of "concentration": difficulty of access for newcomers. To become an "asset manager" requires practically no capital. It requires only the willingness of a few pension fund managers to entrust a newcomer with management of part of their funds. Almost everyone who has earned his spurs with one of the large asset managers and has got to know a few pension funds can therefore open shop for himself.

Indeed, what American asset management today suffers from is "excess of competition." It has become so competitive and so volatile that the participants outdo each other in promising miracles to "beat the market" and to "beat inflation." Both are, of course, impossible. Pension funds cannot beat the market—they are the market. And the history of the past ten years should by now have taught even the most gullible that no one can beat inflation.* It dispossesses everyone except that universal debtor, the government. But because the ability of the asset managers to attract pension fund business heavily depends on their promise to perform such miracles, they tend to concentrate on short-term results: the next ninety days or, perhaps, the next swing in the stock market. Yet, by definition, pensions are long-term. Pension fund management therefore requires long-term strategies for true performance. It is an axiom proven countless times that a series of short-term tactics, no matter how brilliant, will never add up to a successful long-term strategy.

The real problem posed by the shift of the capital market to the pension funds and their asset managers is a far more serious one than "excessive concentration of economic power," even if there were such a thing. The capital market decisions are effectively shifting from the "entrepreneurs" to the "trustees," from the people who are supposed to invest in the future to the people who have to follow the "prudent man rule," which means, in effect, investing in past performance. Herein lies a danger of starving the new, the young, the small, the growing business. But this is happening at a time when the need for new businesses is particularly urgent, whether they are based on new technology or engaged in converting social and economic needs into business opportunities. Whether the American economy will grow or not, we face a rapid aging of those businesses which were the "new" businesses of the post-

*Not even by owning gold, it seems, and I suspect not even by owning Picassos.

World War II period. And if the American economy does not grow, the rate of obsolescence of existing businesses and, with it, the need to find and finance new businesses will be even greater. Non-growth means hard times and greater pressure for all declining businesses or industries.

Yet we are organizing a capital market totally unequipped to supply entrepreneurial capital needs. It is not only that, as "prudent men" and "trustees," the asset managers of the pension funds are debarred from entrepreneurial investment. Temperamentally they are the wrong people for the job. It requires quite different skills and different rules to invest in the old and existing as opposed to new ventures. The person who is investing in what already exists is, in effect, trying to minimize risk. He invests in established trends and markets, in proven technology and management performance. The entrepreneurial investor, on the other hand, must make the most of all opportunities without much regard to risk. To be at all successful, he must operate on the assumption that out of ten investments seven will go sour and have to be liquidated with more or less total loss. Of the remainder, two will not do too poorly—but at best only well enough to offset the seven failures. Perhaps one (with the odds against this very high) will be a "star": a new Xerox, a new IBM, or a new MacDonald's hamburger chain. There is no way to judge in advance which of ten investments in the young and the new will turn out failures and which will succeed. No amount of analysis or "research" does much good, for one cannot analyze or research something that does not yet exist, something that is still promise rather than performance. The entrepreneurial skill does not lie in "picking investments." It lies in knowing what to abandon because it fails to pan out, and what to push and support with full force because it "looks right" despite some initial setbacks.

The problems of the small but growing business, while different, are also dissimilar from those of the established big or fair-sized business. They require a different investment policy, different relationships to management, and a different understanding of business economics, management, and dynamics.

A "trustee" is not entitled to make such investments in the new or the small business, even if he knew how to make them well. Yet if they are not made, the economy will ossify. What is needed, therefore, are new capital market institutions specifically provided to give these new, young, growing businesses the capital (and the management guidance) they need; and which, at the same time, can act as investment vehicles suited for the fiduciary, the asset-manager trustee. Such institutions can develop what the asset manager badly needs: a proven "track record" of performance over a five- or ten-year period. At the same time, they can aggregate in their portfolios the mix of successful and unsuccessful investments which entrepreneurial investment must imply, and can therefore provide the asset manager with the investment vehicle he can use.

Such institutions are not unknown. Europe's leading commercial bank, the Deutsche Bank in Germany, was started well over 100 years ago to be such a financial entrepreneur. Between the two world wars, the United Dominion Corporation in Great Britain played, successfully, a similar role. In this country, Georges Doriot, for many years Professor of Manufacturing at the Harvard Business School, started before World War II what is now American Research and Development Corporation—the father, or at least godfather, of many of the "high technology" companies that have sprung up in the Boston area these last twenty-five years.

Now, however, such entrepreneurial investors must be

created systematically, to serve both the American economy and the new capital market of the pension funds. Above all, we need a commitment on the part of the large pension funds to put aside a small but significant share of their assets (perhaps 10 percent) for investment in such entrepreneurial investors. So far, pension fund management is still trying to guess what the stock market will do in six months time.

The Erosion of Capital Formation

What is being paid into the pension account of an individual represents "savings" to him. But it is not "capital formation." Rather, it is a "transfer payment," taking away consumer purchasing power and transferring it to a retired worker who, of course, will almost always spend every penny of it on consumption.

Social Security contributions, from the beginning, were pure "transfer payments." Every penny paid into Social Security accounts went out immediately as government spending. What Social Security called "reserves" were simply government IOU's for money spent.

Corporate pension funds have been forming capital and are still doing so. They have been taking in more money so far than they have had to pay out as pensions; and the excess of income has become truly "productive investment," as a rule. But any retirement fund is bound to reach a balance between income and outgo within thirty to forty years, if not sooner. Then the youngest employee at the time the fund started approaches retirement age and thus becomes a "dissaver." For the past ten or fifteen years—the period of their lusty infancy—the corporate pension funds have been one of the two agencies of genuine capital formation in the United States, matched only by industry's retained earnings. For another ten years they will still form capital—though at a diminishing rate—in the range of $20 billion a year or between 1 and 2 percent of personal income. By 1990 at the latest they will have become transfer mechanisms, even if their total assets still grow.

Indeed, by that time the pension funds are likely to bring about negative capital formation. As more and more of the beneficiaries age and begin to draw retirement benefits, the funds will increasingly need cash income rather than capital gains. They will need dividends, in other words, and will have to put pressure on the companies they own to increase dividend pay-out and to decrease retained earnings—and with them capital formation. It is well known that the U.S. economy has the lowest rate of "true savings," that is, capital formation, of any developed nation except Canada.* The explanation for this apparent paradox is that most of what the individual considers "savings" is economically speaking "consumption" or, at best, "pseudo-savings."

One reason for this high individual, and low economic, savings rate is America's high housing standard and high rate of home ownership. The residential home, while an

---

*The rate of U.S. savings available for investment is actually lower than the reported 7½ to 9 percent of personal income. For the U.S. has for forty years made up the deficiency in Canada's savings; one-sixth or so of U.S. savings, or 1 to 1½ percent, were used to finance Canada and to create Canadian jobs rather than to finance the U.S. itself. While investment needs in Canada are higher than in the U.S., savings rates have been kept artificially low by a long-standing Canadian governmental policy which pushes up consumption at the expense of savings. In Canada today there is a great deal of talk about "limiting" or "excluding" U.S. investment. The real economic problem of Canada will surely be how to prevent a sharp drop in U.S. investment now that the U.S., as a result largely of pension fund socialism, will suffer a long-term capital shortage. Canada—like the U.S.—has the financial resources to increase personal savings sharply. But so far she has neither the political will to do so nor the necessary capital market institutions.

"asset" for the individual, is economically speaking "durable consumer good" rather than "productive investment." It has a "trade-in value," but no "wealth-producing capacity"; it is not "capital." Another reason is Social Security, which now amounts to 10 percent of wage income (plus 2 percent paid jointly by employer and employee for health care after age sixty-five). Again, this is "savings" for the individual but "transfer payment" for the economy. And the private pension plans add to this another 7 to 9 percent of wage income, of which 2 percent today still represents genuine "savings" and capital formation—but not for very much longer.

Altogether, the "individual savings rate" in this country (including housing) thus approaches 30 percent of personal income. This is what the individual considers savings, and it includes mortgage payments on the house, Social Security, life insurance, and private pension plan contribution. The economist talks of a 7 to 9 percent "personal savings rate"; but he includes the pension plan contribution by or on behalf of the individual, which runs close to 7 to 9 percent of income; the true personal savings ratio therefore approaches zero. This leaves only the retained earnings of business for capital investment, which at their very highest run to no more than 3 to 4 percent of gross national products; total business earnings after taxes reach 5 percent of GNP only in exceptionally profitable years, and dividends must be paid, after all. But a 3 to 4 percent rate of capital formation is well below what is needed for replacement alone, leaving nothing over for additions to the stock of capital.

Yet we face a period of very high demand for new capital: for energy, for the environment, for a railroad system drained of capital, for the inner city, and also for increased productivity in agriculture to feed a hungry world. And for another five years we also will have to create 1 to 1.5 million new jobs every year to take care of the babies of the baby boom of the fifties. Each job in the American economy requires an average capital investment of $40,000 to $100,000 or more.

Demographics rather than the pension funds are at the root of the problem. We now have to support one older person—retired or "survivor"—for every three of working age. Were this money spent on their support available instead for genuine capital formation, there would be no problem at all. In fact, we would probably "oversave" with our present rate of "personal" or "pseudo-savings." But while the pension funds are not the cause of the squeeze, capital formation is going to be a fundamental and permanent problem of pension fund socialism. Indeed, it may be *the* economic problem of pension fund socialism. For the belief that contributions to Social Security and pension plans are "savings" tends quite understandably to cut down sharply on the economy's total propensity to save. It thus creates a permanent tendency toward "undersaving" rather than the "oversaving" which Keynes and the Keynesians postulated as the normal tendency for a developed "capitalist" economy. It is also something quite different from the "undersaving" of the classical economists (including Marx), which always referred to "personal savings."

There are enormous implications here, both theoretical and practical, to which no one seems to have given much thought so far—another indication, by the way, of the folly of our complacency over the pension funds and their consequences. The theoretical implications are startling though simple. If pension fund socialism has a built-in tendency toward undersaving, then policies to stimulate consumption can have one and only one result: further inflation. And they will do so regardless of economic conditions, in a depression as well as in a boom, in times of idle resources and unemployment as well as in times of high plant utilization and full employment. The only effective economic policy, especially in a recession, would be one that stimulates genuine capital formation—diverting resources from consumption into productive investment.

This is not as novel a conclusion as it may sound. The great Austro-American economist Joseph Schumpeter anticipated it, first in a 1918 essay on the "Fiscal State" and then in his later writings, especially his classic *Capitalism, Socialism and Democracy.* * More recently, the Canadian economist Robert A. Mundell, now at Columbia, has reached very similar conclusions, based on twenty years study of the world economy and of the impact of traditional monetary policies on prices and incomes.† Still, it is a conclusion that is totally at odds with classical, pre-Keynesian economics, with Marxist economics, and with the now dominant Keynesian and post-Keynesian (e.g., Milton Friedman's) economics. It does not, as did classical economics, assume "Say's Law," which expects automatic market forces to maintain a self-regulating balance between savings, consumption, and investment. But also, in sharp contrast to Marxist economics, it does not consider "capital" a political "rip-off" of the "system"; rather, it treats it as a fundamental "factor of production," the necessary cost of the future of *any* economic system, be it cave man, capitalist, or Communist.‡ It does not assume, with either the Keynesians or Friedman, that savings are a function of "macroeconomics," e.g., government deficits or money supply,

*(New York: Harper & Row, 1946).

†See the article, "The Mundell-Laffer Hypothesis," by Jude Wanniski, in *The Public Interest,* Spring 1975.

‡Something, it should be said, that has been tacitly accepted by all latter-day Marxists, including Communist planners, since the German "revisionists" around 1900.

which the government economy can unilaterally manipulate. The conclusion further implies that pension fund socialism is structurally different from the "mature capitalist economy" of the Keynesians. What makes it different is precisely that "personal savings," largely as a result of the pension fund mechanism, are no longer "capital fund" and "savings" but "transfer payments" and "consumption."

The practical implications are equally radical. The central problem of American economic policy will have to be the stimulation of genuine savings so as to attain the minimum rate of genuine capital formation—maybe 12 to 15 percent of personal income—needed for economic maintenance, let alone for economic growth at least at the same rate as pension-force growth.

There are only three ways of achieving this. One is to increase personal savings over and above the present rate of "pseudo-savings," i.e., savings for residential homes, Social Security, and private pension plans. Clearly this would be the best way to increase capital formation; it would also be the easiest way in terms of institutions since the pension funds are ready-made vehicles for receiving and handling additional savings. An employee could be encouraged to add additional amounts above the standard contribution into his pension account—and now that vesting is mandatory after ten years, the individual employee will have an account in his name once he has reached the vesting stage.

Again, Teachers Insurance & Annuity Association has pioneered the solution and proven its feasibility. Any holder of an annuity account at TIAA can at any time make an additional individual payment into his or her account that will simply be added to the annual contribution he and his employer make under the TIAA contract. Under existing law this extra contribution is not tax-deferred but comes out of income after taxes; once paid in, these amounts will not be returned, nor can there be any borrowing against them. They are blocked until the payor starts drawing retirement benefits, unless he dies first. Even so, a very large number of TIAA annuity holders regularly make substantial extra payments.*

The TIAA experience indicates that the willingness to increase savings, even in an inflationary period, exists or could be stimulated fairly easily. What is lacking are incentives to save. Indeed, American economic policy, under neo-Keynesian influence, has almost been hostile to savings and has done everything to stimulate consumption. This can no longer be considered a rational policy, let alone the right one.

The second way to increase the true rate of capital formation is to increase the share of capital—whether interest payments or corporate profits—in the nation's gross national product. This is the solution toward which market forces would tend to push us. Under pension fund socialism the costs of capital will tend to rise anyhow. With "savings" going into "transfer payments," genuine capital—and money altogether—must become dearer. But politically this would be a difficult solution; it would also be painful, especially for small or new businesses which have no retained earnings to generate funds internally. A less painful way to the same end would, of course, be the abolition or sharp reduction of the tax on capital formation, that is, the corporation income tax. The $40 billion collected in

*TIAA publishes no figures and, rightly, considers such information confidential. But a sampling of the faculties of several institutions with TIAA contracts would indicate that a majority of faculty members, beginning with fairly young and moderately paid ones, *regularly* make extra payments of significant size into their individual TIAA accounts. And so, apparently, do a good many hospital employees with TIAA pension contracts, even though their incomes are often lower than those of college faculty.

a year of record earnings as tax on corporations constitutes only one sixth of federal tax income. But this is equal to the *entire* amount now available from all sources for genuine capital formation. If released by government most of this money would become capital investment.

The third way is forced saving, such as the Soviet "turnover tax," which is in effect a 50 to 100 percent gross profit margin and a tax on consumption to provide the capital for the Russian economy. This is a wasteful way to form capital; profit margins in Russia have to be several times those of a market economy. It means very low productivity of capital, and would, of course, hardly be compatible with the survival of free institutions. As long as a government remains under the control of an electorate, it is most unlikely to be permitted to form capital; whatever it takes in (except maybe for short war-time periods) becomes consumption through "transfer payments." If we have to resort to compulsory levies to form the minimum of capital needed, the "decentralized market socialism"—and democracy altogether—will have failed; and the private pension system will go down the drain with them. But compulsory capital formation by a dictatorial, if not a totalitarian, régime is the last resort if all else fails.

We have so far given almost no thought in this country to the ways in which capital formation could be increased to offset the actual "dissaving" resulting from the rise of pension costs, which springs in turn from the growth in the number of older retired people whose consumption has to be financed out of the "pseudo-savings" of employed workers. One thing only can be said with certainty: obstacles to, and penalties on, capital formation are a luxury which a society under pension fund socialism—and a society in which a large number of older people have to be supported in retirement—can ill afford. A mixture of incentives for savings, higher costs of capital and, one may hope, lower taxes and lower penalties on capital formation, would probably be the most effective approach. But it is futile to predict what we will do, indeed even whether we will do anything sensible, and in time.

But one can say definitely that capital formation rather than consumption will of necessity become the central problem of domestic economic policy in the years ahead, and the acid test of the economic viability of America's pension fund socialism, if not altogether of her free institutions.

The Political Problems of Pension Fund Socialism

Just as the rise of pension fund socialism has revived the old "economic problems" of socialism, it has also revived the old "political problems" of socialism, and especially the problem of governance and structure of the autonomous, self-governing social institutions which in any "democratic" socialism would have to shoulder major social tasks.

There is, first, the question of the accountability, control, and legitimacy of the autonomous institutions of the society; and specifically of business and its management.

The emergence of the pension fund makes final the divorce of *traditional* "ownership" from "control," which has been a favorite topic of writers on the industrial and post-industrial economy since Berle and Means's pioneering book, written forty-five years ago.* The pension funds are not "owners," they are investors. They do not want "control"; indeed, they are disqualified from exercising it. The pension funds are "trustees." It is their job to invest the

*A. A. Berle and Gardner C. Means, *The Modern Corporation and Private Property* (New York: Harcourt Brace Jovanovich, 1932).

beneficiaries' money in the most profitable investment. They have no business trying to "manage." If they do not like a company or its management, their duty is to sell the stock. To sit on a board of directors, for instance, and accept the obligations of board membership, is incompatible with the duties as "trustees" which the pension fund managers have to discharge and which have been sharply and strictly defined in the Pension Reform Act of 1974.

Yet this leaves management without anyone to be accountable to, a situation that is clearly intolerable.* It is also a barrier to effective management. Management and the business it manages need an effective board just as much as the new owners of American business, the future pension beneficiaries, and society itself. Management must be accountable to an effective board which represents genuine "constituencies."

There is need to balance in the governance of large enterprises, three main interests or constituencies served: the consumer, the present employees, and the "investors," which increasingly means the new owners (i.e., the beneficiaries of the pension funds). American management must be faulted for neglecting the consumer interest during the long years of the consumption boom following World War II. It can be accused of supporting instead a cabal of investors and workers, and with it one-sided domination by the "producer interests." For the sake of labor peace—which society evidently wanted and indeed demanded—management was willing to make over to the employee the *entire* increase in wealth generated by new technology, higher capital investment, and increased productivity. Labor's share in the national income rose steadily as the employee got a larger share of the larger pie. The investor's share

*See Chapter 52, "Needed, an Effective Board," in my recent book, *Management: Tasks, Responsibilities, Practices* (New York: Harper & Row, 1974).

shrank, but only slowly, at least until the inflationary years of the late sixties. Management strategy, in other words, was to favor the "producer interest," with the only issue being which of the two groups of producers should get more—an issue that labor won almost every time. But none or few of the benefits of increased productivity of higher capital investment or of the new technology were passed on to the consumer.

This neglect of the consumer interest may, of course, be blamed on union leadership rather than on management. But management knew very well in theory that it had to do what it failed to do: represent the consumer. The "total marketing approach," which had become the fashion in management circles after World War II, preached that management had, above all, to represent the consumer interests; but this was rarely practiced. In this sense "consumerism" can be considered a predictable reaction, and might be called (as I have said several times) the "shame of marketing."

If management now defaults similarly on its duties to the constituency of its new "owners"—that is, the pension fund beneficiaries—it will lose legitimacy and, predictably soon, autonomy too. It will come to be dominated by the one organized powerful interest, that of the present employees and their unions. But the unions are incapable of controlling management; and they are quite unlikely to be considered as legitimate centers of management power by American society. Sooner or later central government—society's universal receiver in political bankruptcy—will be called in to restore the balance, which can only mean that management loses its autonomy and decision-making power altogether to government control and government representatives.

Every single pension contract implies a social responsibility on the part of business to produce a surplus adequate to support its former (now retired) employees. This in turn demands understanding and support on the part of the employees of America of management and its responsibility for productivity. For management alone makes resources productive. But how can management create this understanding and obtain the necessary support on the part of its new owners?

Business has to establish an effective relationship with its new owners in order to protect its autonomy—and with it the interest of these owners—against rapacious governments, against tax policies inimical to economic growth and performance or to the future income security of the new owners, and against policies (whether originating with government or with labor) which are inflationary and therefore a direct assault on the long-term interests of the new owners as pension fund beneficiaries.

Equally important is the opportunity that faces business management today. The emergence of the pension funds as the new owners of American business does represent a unique opportunity to restore the legitimacy of management. This is an "ownership" interest which society *will* accept as legitimate. At the same time, the interest of these owners and the interest of the enterprise are identical, which is not necessarily always the case for the two other constituencies, those of present workers and of consumers.

How can this identity of interests between the enterprise and the new owners be made into overt institutional reality?

The Pension Funds as Institutions

The new institutions that we have created—the pension funds and their "asset managers," who administer and invest the pension monies—must have adequate management and be rendered legitimate. Further, they must represent the beneficiaries and bear a clear-cut relationship to them. The pension funds have to be autonomous institutions. They have to be accountable. They must be able to communicate with their constituencies—the people for whom they are trustees. Otherwise, as can be predicted with near-certainty, the first major "scandal" will bring about a plan for government regulation and eventually government takeover. By and large, however, the corporate pension funds and asset managers have not yet even begun to organize themselves for either accountability or legitimacy.

These new institutions must be free from any suspicion of conflict of interests. They must be set up to serve their beneficiaries and no one else. By historical accident, the bulk of asset management is today concentrated in a fairly small number of commercial banks, above all in New York City, the trust departments of which manage the largest and most important corporate pension funds. The benefit of this to the banks is, at most, marginal. In the banking industry itself it is said that only a half dozen or so commercial banks—even among the hundred largest ones—make money out of pension fund management; those few only started to make money quite recently and do not make a great deal either. But whether pension fund management is profitable for the commercial banks is not the real issue. What matters is that being both commercial banker and pension fund manager puts the bank into an inherent conflict of interests.

When the Penn Central collapsed in 1970, several of the big banks, especially Chase Manhattan in New York, were severely criticized. Their loan officers were said to have told their colleagues in the bank's trust department who were running major pension funds, of the critical condition of the railroad. Thereupon the trust department sold its customers' holdings in Penn Central, thus "trading on insider knowledge." To make sure that this cannot happen again, all the major banks handling pension fund assets have built a so-called Chinese Wall between their commercial lending operations and their trust departments to prevent any "leaks." But this is a worse breach of trust than the leak itself. For as a fiduciary, the bank—and it is the bank, not the trust department, that is the contracting party in law and equity—*must* use its knowledge to protect its trustors. Had the Pension Reform Act of 1974 been in force when the Penn Central collapsed, any corporation whose pension fund was managed by a commercial bank with inside knowledge of the railroad's plight which did *not* use this knowledge in its pension fund management could have sued for breach of trust and demanded heavy damages. Indeed, under the Pension Reform Act of 1974 the corporation's managers probably would have a legal duty to sue the bank, or be liable to heavy damages themselves.

All told, acting as both commercial banker and asset manager does the bank more harm than good. It creates suspicion among its corporate clients. During the "credit crunch" of 1973–74 many corporate treasurers came to believe that in granting a loan—a decision on which the very survival of the company often depended—the banks favored companies willing to give them their pension fund business. The banks deny this heatedly, probably with justice in most cases. But a fiduciary has to avoid even the suspicion of a conflict of interests or he cannot be trusted. Similarly, the New York City banks found themselves in a conflict of interest between their pension fund responsibility and their role as underwriters for the City's bonds in New York City's financial crisis of 1975—again an untenable position for a trustee.

Pension funds are much too important to be run as a sideline, which is all they can or should be in a commercial bank. Pension fund management requires and deserves an independent institution, divorced from commercial banking, investment banking, or any other banking business. In Canada the banks long ago put trust activities into separate trust companies. The trust company still uses the data-processing facilities of a major commercial bank (which an asset manager could duplicate only at substantial cost) while paying for these services through the deposits it maintains in the bank for its own needs. These trust companies are separately incorporated businesses, with their own offices and managements. This is hardly the model for the United States; the Canadian Trust Company is a far more limited institution than the strong, powerful, and aggressively run asset managers that America's pension fund socialism requires. But the Canadian example shows that commercial banking and fiduciary work can be separated without hurting either.

All this is so obvious that one can predict that pension fund management will be divorced from commercial banking fairly soon. It is indeed rumored that several of the country's leading banks are already studying how and when to take the step. It would surely be more intelligent for the banks to act on their own initiative than to wait until government forces them to do so. But setting up pension fund management as an autonomous institution would only be the first step. It is equally important that pension funds be organized for accountability and legitimacy.

The thorniest of the problems of authority, legitimacy, and control of the pension funds is the one problem for which the old course in "The Problems of Socialism" never had an answer, except for pious hopes: How to protect the integrity of the pension fund assets against rapacious governments who raid such funds to stuff governmental coffers and finance governmental irresponsibility. This is certain to become a central problem of American pension fund socialism.

Indeed, such raiding is already under way. In the first act of the tragicomedy of financing New York City in the summer of 1975, two of the pension funds of New York City's own employees were "persuaded" to take $125 millions of the City's new notes. Four weeks later, in Act II, another four pension funds of city employees were pressured into taking $165 millions. This then became $750 million in City bonds, to be bought by the pension funds of City employees. And in November, the pension funds of New York City and New York State employees found themselves finally saddled with a total of $3 billions in new City bonds of dubious value which no one else was willing to buy. A little earlier, in August 1975, two of the City's five borough presidents and the City council president proposed emergency legislation to force pension plans of companies with offices in New York City to put a large portion of their assets into City obligations which were clearly not "creditworthy," in fact, were barely pious hopes. Apparently, it did not occur to these distinguished statesmen that every business that could possibly do so (i.e., every business except the hotels and the local utility companies) would promptly move out of of New York City, rendering the City's collapse final and irreversible.

The Social Security system is also in considerable financial straits, largely because, as in New York City, it is making "welfare" payments rather than payments of Social Security pensions to retired persons or to the survivors of insured workers whose payroll deductions finance the Social Security system. No wonder that some congressional staffers and other government "experts" have suggested tapping the private pension funds for investment in Social Security "obligations," in other words, raiding the private pension funds to finance government deficits.

Many businesses—and not only international corporations—would respond to such a measure by leaving the country, making their U.S. business into a subsidiary. If one can move one's headquarters from the Inner City to the Connecticut exurbia, one might, after all, move them to Prince Edward Island or to Brussels as well. Many more businesses would cut back on their American activities. A foreign company would be singularly foolish to set up operations in the United States if that meant incurring pension liabilities to its American employees while having its pension assets confiscated. Still, economic reality by itself has not always been an adequate defense against governmental greed or demagoguery.

No quicker way to destroy the pension fund system could be devised than to make it a source of compulsory levies. And no quicker way could be devised to make sure that tomorrow's pensioners would not receive the pensions they pay for today. Of course, under today's law the trustee of a corporate pension fund who bought New York City obligations when the City was bankrupt and yet unwilling to take the steps necessary to restore its solvency would be clearly violating his legal duty. And so would anyone buying government obligations to finance the Social Security deficit. A clearer breach of the prudent man rule which pension fund managers are legally obligated to observe could hardly be imagined. But the same Congress that wrote the Pension Reform Act of 1974 could, after all, change the act. An innocuous-sounding amendment requiring pension funds to invest a certain proportion of their assets in specifically designated government securities would, in all probability, have wide popular support, even from its main victims, the future pension fund recipients.

How can this be prevented? Perhaps the only effective safeguard is public vigilance, a proper understanding on the part of the country's employees, and especially of the labor unions, that the pension funds are *their* assets and that they have a vital stake in their political autonomy and financial integrity. Again, the building up of such understanding and support on the part of the new owners emerges as a crucial but unfulfilled need.

The Reforms Needed

The first priority for both business and pension funds is to establish boards of directors and trustees which can satisfy three requirements. Their tasks must be:

(1) to provide the effective organ of control and accountability that business and pension funds must have.
(2) to provide representation of the "constituencies," and especially of the new "owners."
(3) to reach the new "owners," the country's employees, and obtain their understanding and support.

The first step—but only the first—is the appointment of "professional" directors, men or women of public standing and proven competence who, as members of the board, can be truly independent of management.* A board led by such directors would not merely have the right but the clear duty to replace a management that did not live up to its respon-

*As I proposed in *Management: Tasks, Responsibilities, Practices,* this professional director would have to be of proven executive capacity; well under retirement age himself; limited to four or five directorships; paid adequately so that the total income from all his directorships would equal the pay of a senior executive; and limited probably in his term of office to six years or so, without being immediately eligible for re-election, so that he is truly independent of management. He would also have to be a full-time professional director, without other work or profession.

sibilities and to stringent performance standards. It would thus wield the same powers as yesterday's "director," representing yesterday's "owners" (the "capitalists") held and exercised.

But, in addition, both business and pension fund need what, for want of a better name, I have been calling a public and community relations board, that is, strong, visible membership on the board by people who represent both true "constituencies," such as consumers and employers, and the future new "owners"—the country's employees. The pension fund of any given company is owned by that company's employees, for whom the fund itself acts as trustee and financial manager. But the pension fund, in turn, owns other companies; and the major pension funds collectively own a large percentage of all major businesses. The employee interest as the genuine ownership interest of business therefore has to be represented strongly on each company board. And the business in turn, as well as its pension fund, requires a direct relationship to these owners.

This may sound a bold innovation. Yet the country's oldest "industry-wide" pension fund created such a "public and community relations board" fifty years ago. Since its founding by the Carnegie Foundation in the early twenties, Teachers Insurance and Annuity Association has had a board of distinguished university administrators and academic economists, elected by and representing the "constituents," the country's private universities and their faculties. Most American managements still consider such a board "far out."

Pension fund socialism should make it possible for management to regain legitimacy precisely because it re-establishes a genuine, socially anchored ownership. This in turn necessitates a radical restructuring of the institution of governance: the board of directors or trustees.

Yet such restructuring alone, however radical it may seem, would still not satisfy the third, and perhaps most important, of our requirements: that business and pension fund reach the new owners and obtain their understanding and support. Here more will be needed than an institutional change; what is entailed is no less than a change in the entire pension fund structure.

The great majority of American pension funds· are "investment funds" in the way they manage their assets. They invest in the American economy. Indeed, as Charles Wilson of GM saw clearly a quarter century ago, this is the only way to fund a universal pension system. Even if we nationalized pensions entirely and made them a government monopoly, there would be no other way. If every three working adults have to support one older retired person or survivor, even at a lower standard of living, the support base must be as broad as the economy itself, consisting of the surplus of current production over the consumption of the people at work, in other words, the business profits of the economy. In that respect the pensions paid to retired people in the Soviet Union are financed exactly the same way we finance pensions under private plans in the United States, out of business profits obtained in the form of the "turnover tax."

But for most workers the pension plan is still an "annuity" plan. In the great majority of American pension plans, the employee is guaranteed a fixed-money income independent of the profitability of the businesses in which the fund's assets are invested or of the stock market price of their securities. Typically, this guaranteed income is based on the employee's earnings during the last years of his employment—though increasingly with some adjustment for inflation.

This means that the employer has to pay a large contribution to the company pension plan if stock prices or dividends go down. But he pays less if either or both go up. This was indeed one reason why companies during the fifties and especially the sixties favored the GM plan. In those "go-go years" it was widely hoped that an ever-rising stock market, rather than the company itself, would provide the pension money. Yet to base an annuity plan on an "investment fund" is the wrong policy from the company's point of view, since it means that companies have to raise their contributions to the pension plan just when they can least afford it, in lean times. Most American companies found that out, of course, in the last few years when the collapse of the "go-go market" forced them to increase their pension fund contribution just when their own revenues and profits went down sharply.

For the economy, too, the present system is harmful. It is in poor times that business most needs liquidity, retained earnings, and capacity to invest; and it is in poor times that business, for the sake of the economy, most needs to hold on to earnings, when the capacity of business to maintain capital investment becomes the critical factor. Our present pension system sharply curtails this capacity, while encouraging investment in boom times when it should actually be curtailed. The current system—quite unintentionally though—aggravates the fluctuations in the business cycle.

For the employee, too, the present system has serious drawbacks. It bases his retirement expectation on a fixed-money "annuity" plan while funding it entirely through an "investment fund," primarily via equity investment. In the first place, this is really not what he wants. Whenever employees are offered an opportunity to invest in the economy in the form of equity investments, they eagerly avail themselves of it. They may be wrong in believing that in the long run common stock investments, especially if managed knowledgeably, are a better investment than such fixed-value investments as bonds or mortgages; the evidence is by no means conclusive. But they are surely right in believing that in the long run inflation is more likely than deflation; and common stock, while by no means immune to it, does offer a little more protection against inflation. Above all, they believe that the "owner" will in the end always get a better deal than the "creditor" (except in an actual liquidation following final bankruptcy). And this belief—however inconsistent it may be with the Protestant ethic—the economic history of the United States and of most other countries, East or West, would fully tend to support.

That this fact is rarely acknowledged is the result, in large part, of equating the term "employee" with "blue-collar worker," if not with "laborer." Maybe, as unions traditionally maintain, "laborers" should not invest in common stock—though the "laborers" themselves clearly do not share this belief. But, of course, the participants in the pension funds are predominantly not blue-collar workers, let alone laborers. They are the American work force, in which blue-collar workers are by now a distinct and shrinking minority. Of the 90 million people in the American work force of 1975, no more than one-third was classified as "blue-collar," even if farmers are counted as such; roughly two-fifths worked as managers, professionals, or technicians, with another fifth working as highly skilled and well-paid craftsmen. By 1985 the blue-collar group will be a good deal smaller. Where employment in manufacturing in 1975 still accounted for almost a quarter (23 percent) of the labor force, it may have shrunk to 15 percent by the late eighties; some observers even predict that it will be down to 5 percent, roughly the same proportion farmers hold now. And managers, professionals, and technicians will almost certainly become the majority group in the work force within ten to fifteen years; the educational system alone ensures the continuing shift from "manual work," skilled or unskilled, to "knowledge work," skilled or unskilled.

The "knowledge worker" already represents a majority among the future pension fund beneficiaries, those people under thirty-five or forty whose contributions support the ones who are on pensions today or will go on pensions in the next few years. It is this future pension fund beneficiary who has the greatest stake in both the performance and the integrity of the pension funds.

The incomes of these knowledge workers in the pension plans tend to be well above the national income average, if only because the very poorest groups—the bottom fifth of the population of working age—tend not to be enrolled in any pension program except, marginally, in Social Security. Very few of them are highly paid, let alone rich, nor is their financial sophistication very great. Yet in both income level and information they are a far cry indeed from the "laborer" or even the "machine tender" for whose protection against his own ignorance an "annuity" plan is allegedly needed. And, to repeat, this "employed" (or self-employed) middle class has, in the United States at least, shown a clear preference for equity investment of part of its savings. These people are entitled to some say in how their largest asset, their pension expectation, is to be invested; they should surely be given the option to invest a part of their pension reserve directly, in an account kept in their own name in a professionally managed investment portfolio.

But the employee does not, indeed cannot, escape the downside risks of an investment-based pension fund, or for that matter of any universal pension system. In the event of a serious prolonged downturn in the economy, pensions will go down regardless of the contractual basis. The economy then simply cannot produce the goods and services to live up to its pension promises. Either the purchasing power of fixed-income pensions will be eroded by inflation, or pension contracts will have to be renegotiated. If everyone has a pension claim to the proceeds of the entire economy, no one can expect to escape the effects of a general prolonged downturn in economic activity or stock market values, whatever the fine print in the contract. Under the present system the employee bears the risk; only indirectly, however, if at all, does he benefit from the gain. If times are good, his pension payments may go up because the wages on which annual pension payments are based go up. But a higher stock market benefits only the employer. And in an inflationary era one can no longer expect that the reduction in the money amount of the pension that is inevitable in depression times will be offset by lower prices for the goods and services the retired worker has to buy.

The greatest weakness of the present system is, however, not economical but psychological and political. The employees own American business; but they do not know it, do not perceive it, do not experience it. Indeed, under the present system it is very difficult for them to do so. They know that they have a pension claim; and now, with vesting compulsory, at least for private pension plans, many of them receive an annual report on their own individual pension account. But they do not know what is behind this asset —increasingly their biggest asset, especially for working people past age forty or forty-five. They therefore do not know what measures and policies are in their own interest to protect their most important asset, or what measures and policies endanger it. They cannot act rationally in their own self-interest. They cannot control the business management of pension funds even though they are the owners. In turn, they are rendered incapable of providing the informed support which business management and pension funds need, if only to protect the employees' future livelihood against depredation and raiding.

Twenty-five years ago, quite a few people saw this and warned against an exclusive reliance on annuity (i.e., fixed-income pensions) when investment, of necessity, had to be in the productive, wealth-producing capacity of the economy—and that means in equity. But the contrary arguments then won the day. There was the cogent one that low-income earners—and that was of course the group which everyone then saw as the main, if not the only, beneficiary of company pension plans—could not afford to "speculate." Widows and orphans, the old argument goes, have no business owning common stock. But the unions then also would have opposed any plan other than an annuity plan precisely because it would have forged an overt link between worker pensions and corporate performance and profits. Many corporate managements at the time also liked the annuity plan for the same reason; higher profits and, above all, higher stock prices would not, as they saw it, raise the workers' take but they would reduce the company's pension liability.

No one anticipated long-term inflation. Above all, in those years almost no one could envisage anything except a plan that was either entirely "annuity" or entirely "investment," one in which the pension payment is determined in its entirety by fluctuating profits and depends on fluctuating stock prices. If these are the only choices, then an annuity plan is indeed more prudent and definitely preferable.

Today, however, we know that this is a false choice; there is a middle way combining the advantages of both extremes. It was actually developed at around the time of

GM's plan, and by the same pension fund that had been pioneering all along, the Teachers Insurance and Annuity Association. Up to that time, the TIAA pension plan had been purely an annuity one, although of course a large part of the assets consisted of common stock investments. Then TIAA developed a double-barreled plan. The annuity plan remained the basis; indeed, every participant is required to enroll in it. But he also has the option of putting a portion of his contribution—up to 50 percent of the total—in a straight investment fund (called CREF for College Retirement Equities Fund) which handles a diversified stock market portfolio. The contribution made jointly by the participant's employer and the employee remains the same: a fixed portion of the employee's salary.

This is the key to the problem that had eluded everyone before. For the portion put into the annuity plan the employee receives a fixed-money annuity, based on the contributions made by him and, on his behalf, by his employer. But for the CREF portion of his account he receives an annuity, based on the stock market value of his share of the total CREF portfolio on the day on which he begins to draw his retirement pay.

The great majority of TIAA participants (TIAA enrolls more people than any but the AT&T fund and the very large governmental funds) have availed themselves of the CREF option, many of them to the maximum extent. During the fifties and sixties, CREF did very well. In the last five years, obviously, it has done as poorly as the stock market. Yet the participants who chose to put 50 percent of their pension money into CREF for the last twenty years still have done better than those who stayed entirely in the annuity fund. More important: despite the stock market collapse since 1969–70 very few TIAA participants have switched out of CREF, although a casual chat in the faculty lounge will quickly reveal that they are well aware of the shrinkage in value of their CREF holdings.

What we need is a change in structure that will help make pension funds conform more closely to economic reality, render them better able to serve both employer and employee, and above all, enable them to satisfy the economic, psychological, and political requirements of pension fund socialism. Contributions into a company's pension fund should remain fixed and based on actuarial foundations (although the provision found in some plans which allows a company to adjust contributions in any one year according to changes in profits, provided the full amount due is paid in over a three-year period, might be used more widely). Until an employee reaches the point where his pension becomes vested, every penny of pension money paid for or by him would go into an annuity plan as it does now. Beyond this, a sum adequate to provide for a pre-set minimum pension income including Social Security (say two-fifths of the employee's salary) would be earmarked for the annuity portion of the fund. For all but the most poorly paid workers, this would probably work out at or near 50 percent of the pension fund contribution which TIAA has established as the annuity fund minimum. Beyond this minimum, however, the employee would have the option to put all or any part of the remainder into an "investment fund." If the value of this fund goes up, through capital gains, for example, the gain would be his, resulting in a larger pension when he retires. If it goes down, however, the loss would also be his. In other words, not only would he be an owner; he would be treated like one. Yet he would be protected by the annuity character of at least half of his investment against the risk that we have felt traditionally to be unsuitable for widows and orphans. Then the employee would really begin to understand that he was an owner and might come to act like one.

The chances of such structural change may seem slim today. But there is one group that might espouse it: the labor unions, paradoxical though this may sound at first. For such a change offers the best way out of the dilemma (to be discussed later on) which is increasingly going to confront American labor leaders: the conflict between their function as representatives of the employee against the "boss," and their function as representatives of the "bosses' boss," the new owners or the country's employees.

The Future of Social Security

Of all the problems resulting from the convergence of pension fund socialism, the least expected is the obsolescence of Social Security in its present form and scope.

Social Security was founded in the mid-thirties on two principles. First, Social Security would be gradually expanded until it became the universal retirement system for Americans; and for those covered—practically everybody in the end—it would be the only, or at least the principal, source of retirement income other than individual savings. Secondly, Social Security would be "insurance" rather than "welfare": benefits would equal on a probability basis what the employee (together with his employer) paid into his account. The reserves, while totally invested in government bonds, would be actuarially sound. Above all, nothing not strictly considered "old age and survivor" insurance would be permitted to become mixed, whether financially or administratively, with Social Security.

Both principles are still being invoked in Social Security rhetoric. And indeed Social Security now covers virtually all people at work in the United States, whether employed or self-employed (Except federal government employees).

Even the Railroad Retirement Board, which was set up long before Social Security, has been forced by its increasing financial weakness to merge itself into Social Security in effect (albeit not in law, where it continues to be treated as independent). But in reality both principles have been abandoned. Barring another five or ten years of double-digit inflation, which would undermine all pension systems, public and private, Social Security will have become by 1980 the supplementary rather than the primary source of retirement income for the majority of the country's working people reaching retirement age.

At the same time, Social Security is rapidly changing from pure "insurance" to "welfare." The bulk of Social Security payments, of course, still serve the original task of providing "old age and survivor" insurance. But six out of every ten Social Security employees now work on the new "welfare" tasks: Medicare and the massive case load of Supplemental Security Income benefits to the "needy aged, the blind and the disabled," which was transferred from the states to Social Security on January 1, 1974. The bulk of administrative expenses—and this, of course, also means the majority of administrators, supervisors, and clerks—in the Social Security Administration already goes to "problems" and "needs" rather than to "claims" and "rights." Supplemental Security Income payments in 1974 (their first full year under Social Security) accounted for one-twentieth of total disbursements by the Social Security administration, some $3 billion out of a total of almost $70 billion. Supplemental Income clients are just about one-eighth of the total recipients of Social Security checks, 3 million people out of 25 million. But Supplementary Income's administrative expenses of $500 millions came to one-fifth of the total Social Security budget and equaled one-half of the full cost of the "insurance" programs for old age and survivor pensions (the rest going to the Medicare programs). Moreover, it is only a matter of time before Medicaid, the health care program for the "medically indigent," will be shifted to the Social Security administration. There is no other place for it. And the Food Stamp Program—another "welfare" program in deep trouble—may also end up in Social Security.

To abandon the original principles may have been very unwise, but it is accomplished fact. As a result, it may well be the only intelligent and practical solution to carry the development of the last twenty-five years to its logical conclusion by converting Social Security totally from an "insurance" system into a "welfare" program which takes care of the "problems": the one-quarter or so of all workers who cannot build up an adequate retirement account because theirs are poor jobs (low paid and casual rather than steady); the handicapped and disabled; and so on. These "problems" cannot be provided for out of any kind of genuine "insurance." To the extent to which they are being supported, they will be paid for out of general revenues, that is, out of bona fide taxes.

For two-thirds to three-quarters of the work force, Social Security would then become "reinsurance," with the main burden being borne where it is increasingly already borne, by the employer's pension plan. Some pension insurance would, in effect, become compulsory; and some payments into a central governmental fund would have to continue —for health care costs after retirement, for instance, or until the employee has acquired a "vested" claim to retirement benefits. But to the extent to which employers' pension plans provide for a certain minimum income if contributions are continued until retirement (say 50 percent of the income of a family's main wage earner), Social Security payments would either be cut back or waived altogether.

And national policy might clearly establish a preference for providing retirement income through private plans to the fullest extent possible.

Such a reversal of the official policy of the last forty years may seem today to be a political pipe dream. In fact, we already have moved very far down this road—perhaps halfway. While Social Security has been drawn more and more into welfare programs, tax policy has been increasingly favoring private pension plans of all kinds. Money paid into private pension plans is treated as deferred income, on which taxes are payable only when the benefits are being received after retirement. The Social Security contribution of the employee, on the other hand, comes out of income on which the employee pays taxes in full. The employees of non-governmental, non-profit institutions (private universities, for instance, or charitable organizations) have Option III and Option IV (as noted earlier), under which they can defer taxes on large chunks of their income if they pay it into a private pension fund. In the Pension Reform Act of 1974, Congress went even further. It granted self-employed people the right to defer up to 15 percent of their income, or $7,500 a year, provided it be put into a pension plan. And for employees not covered at all by a private pension plan, it provided for a tax deferral of up to $1,500 a year (or 15 percent of income, whichever is smaller) if put into an approved pension plan—the so-called IRA plans (Individual Retirement Accounts).

We will soon go further still. The IRA provision is bound to be liberalized; there is no reason why employed people not covered by a private pension plan should not be able to defer taxes on the same amount of income as the self-employed—up to $7,500 a year. And there is already a good deal of pressure to grant all employed people under a private pension plan the tax deferrals for the employees of non-profit organizations (Option III and Option IV) so that they can set aside additional sums for future retirement. In fact, such liberalization of private pension contributions is the easiest, and politically the most attractive, way to combine tax cuts with an anti-inflationary policy. It would also greatly ease the conflicts within the employee group between those workers who want more cash and those who want a higher pension contribution, thus genuinely alleviating the problems of the unions. Flexibility in pension contribution should further help to counteract the growing resistance against rising Social Security costs. Yet it might make it possible to give the "problems," especially the "old age proletarians," a larger retirement income out of tax revenues than they now receive when in effect subsidized out of the Social Security contributions of the "affluent" majority.

Above all, we are near the point of revolt against Social Security on the part of the only major employee group that can opt out: the employees of state and local governments. State and local governments have the right to enroll their employees under Social Security, and almost all of them have availed themselves of this option. But they are not compelled to be under Social Security as non-governmental employers and the self-employed are. The pension fund burden will go up sharply in state and local governments as past-service liabilities have to be funded. Taxpayers are already balking at paying higher state and local taxes. The employees, therefore, will have to pay a larger and larger share of the pension burden in state and local governments. At the same time Social Security taxes are going up sharply—and threaten to go up even more sharply. If the amount going into Social Security were instead paid into the pension funds of state and local governments, many of them would be financially stable. No wonder that state and local government employees increasingly agitate for leaving Social Security—especially as their benefits under their own pension plans are so high that Social Security adds little while it costs as much as their own plan, if not more. The employees of the State of Alaska have already voted for withdrawal. New York City has given notice of withdrawal by 1978. And Los Angeles County is about to follow suit.

But if the state and local governments pull out, the entire Social Security system becomes untenable, politically as well as financially. It would be next to impossible to deny to the employees of non-governmental institutions, whether businesses, hospitals or universities, the same rights governmental employees have. Also the main opposition to radical reform of the Social Security system, the opposition of the labor movement, would evaporate. And the only thing that really holds up America's Social Security system, despite the rise of the private pension plans, is the unqualified support of labor.

The emergence of the private pension funds as the primary source of retirement income—while at the same time the Social Security system is increasingly turning into "welfare" rather than "insurance"—makes it highly probable that Social Security "reform" will go well beyond a restructuring of the present system. Any attempt at Social Security reform is likely to reopen the whole question of the role of Social Security, a question which the framers of the present system thought they had settled for good and all forty years ago. What we now *pay for* is still largely the system they envisaged, with Social Security "universal." What we actually *get* is a system in which private pension plans carry more and more of the main burden, with Social Security acting in part as "co-insurer" but increasingly as "non-insurer"—a welfare agency for the non-insurables.

The problems discussed here are as much the problems

of demographics as of pension fund socialism. Any society in which a large proportion of the working population survives beyond working age and lives to "retire" faces these dilemmas. But the emergence of the pension funds is precipitating them in this country. They crystallize around the pension funds and will, in large measure, have to be tackled as problems of those funds.

Pension fund socialism and the demographic changes are accomplished facts. They represent genuine success. But the problems of such success have yet to be tackled, and they are formidable. The greatest is surely our complacency and the prevailing lack of awareness of these changes. The problems themselves can be solved—some quite easily. But this requires that they be understood. So far the employees of America do not even realize that they have become true "owners."

There are also dangers to the pension funds, especially if we continue to disregard the emergence of pension fund economics, pension fund politics, and of pension-fund socialism altogether. Unless we, for instance, find a way to prevent the raiding of their assets by predatory or shiftless governments, the pension funds could well be destroyed again. The unsolved questions of capital formation—including fundamental questions of economic and tax policy in a society where demographics convert "personal savings" into "pseudo-savings" and "consumption spending," thus creating a permanent propensity toward undersaving—not only threaten the country's economic growth and stability. By making inflation appear tempting and the easy way out in the short run, they constitute a continuing threat to social stability, to political sanity, to economic performance, and to the performance capacity of the pension funds as well.

The pension funds of this country developed over the

last twenty-five years may therefore still be seriously damaged; they may even be wrecked. But two facts will remain as permanent changes that cannot be undone. The demographic change is one; we will assuredly live in a society in which large numbers of people survive beyond working age and therefore have to be supported out of the product of those at work. The second enduring new reality is the controlling ownership of the country's productive resources by the private pension funds. This cannot now be reversed. The country's productive resources, the equity capital of our major economic institutions, are already "socialized." Pension fund socialism is therefore accomplished fact.

3. Social Institutions and Social Issues Under Pension Fund Socialism

The New Needs

Any shift in the center of demographic gravity changes society, its mood, its temper, its values, as well as its institutions and issues. And a sudden shift—a rare event in social history—has earthquake impact.

The center of demographic gravity lies in that age group of the adult, or at least adolescent, population (starting at around sixteen or so these days) which represents both the largest single age cohort in the population and the fastest-growing one. In 1959, toward the close of the Eisenhower administration, the center of demographic gravity in the United States was around age thirty-nine—the oldest it has ever been in American history. Five years later, when Lyndon Johnson ran against Barry Goldwater for President, the center of demographic gravity in the United States had swung sharply to age seventeen. And for ten or twelve years thereafter, as the babies born in the baby boom between 1948 and 1959 grew out of childhood, the youngest group in the adult population, a group still in school and considered "adolescent" rather than "adult," represented the center of demographic gravity. What form the "youth decade" would take would have been hard to predict in 1959, but a violent and traumatic shock could have been anticipated.

Now, in the mid- and late seventies, we face a similar shift. The babies of the baby boom are grown up. Indeed, the babies born in the first year in which births in America increased sharply (1947–48) are now almost thirty years old. And the youngsters who are entering the age at which they have an impact on the mood, temper, values, problems, and issues of a society—that is, age sixteen or seventeen—are already products of the lean birth years, which began in 1960 and which in a brief spell cut total births in the United States by more than a quarter. The "youth decade" is definitely over.

But, and this is unprecedented, at least in modern history, American society (and that of all other developed countries, to a greater or lesser degree) now faces a period during which there will be *two* centers of demographic gravity. The first will be that of the young adults, the babies of the baby boom of 1948–59 who, by and large, have entered the labor force—or will have done so by 1979. This group will grow from 30 to 40 million in the next ten years, that is, by a full third. The members of this group are forming families and getting started on work and careers. They are therefore entering what in many ways is the most conservative age of man (and especially of woman), the age in which concerns with salary and job, with the mortgage on the home, the pediatrician's bill, and the schooling of one's children tend to predominate. Hardly a month goes by without the publication of some book or article which reports with amazement how "bourgeois" the "fiery radicals" of 1965 had become by the mid-seventies. With equal surprise, the fact that McGovern lost the presidential campaign of 1972 is attributed to the defection of so many former "youth rebels," who voted their "pocketbook" rather than their convictions. But this shift should not occasion surprise. It only reflects the inevitable changes which the transition from adolescence to young adult imposes. For the young adult family must be concerned with things close to home and of direct personal interest, rather than with the so-called big issues.

The second, equally important center of population gravity will consist of the older people past retirement age or approaching it. The number of people over sixty-five and of "survivors," especially widows fifty-five to sixty-five years old, is increasing just as rapidly as the young adults and will soon match them. Now amounting to some 30 millions, they too will reach 40 millions or so by the mid-eighties. This group also, in its own way, is exceedingly "conservative," preoccupied with its own immediate problems and needs rather than the "issues."

After 1985, the center of gravity of the American population will shift steadily toward middle age; and by the late eighties, it will be where it was in the late Eisenhower years when the sharp shift in population dynamics first began—that is, around forty or so. The number of young people entering adulthood each year will go down quite sharply in the mid-eighties, by a quarter or more. The number of old people reaching sixty-five will no longer increase very sharply and will indeed tend to go down in the nineties, as the babies born in the lean birth years of the Great Depression reach retirement age; but the number of older people surviving beyond sixty-five will continue to go up steadily. Unless there is another baby boom—and this would not have an impact on adult population structure until well into the nineties, even if it began now—the center of population gravity in the United States will steadily creep upwards until, after the year 2010, the old people, over sixty-five, will become the main population center as the babies of the baby boom between 1948 and 1959 reach retirement age.

Population trends and population changes will thus for many years have a major impact on society, policies, and politics in America. But sharp changes in institutional structure also have profound impact on society, its issues, problems, and concerns. The emergence of the pension funds as central institutions, as the new channels for capital formation and capital allocation, as the only "capitalists" in America, and as the dominant "owners" of America's productive resources, is as profound a change as are the shifts in the center of demographic gravity.

Both changes are, of course, closely interrelated. The emergence of the pension fund is, after all, the American response to the demographic changes. The two together form the essence of pension fund socialism. And both changes, the demographic and the institutional, will continue to create needs and opportunities, and pose new problems for many decades ahead. This book, however, focuses on the problems of the next ten years, the years until the mid- and late eighties. For it is in these next ten years that basic decisions in respect to America's pension fund socialism will have to be made.

That there will be profound changes is certain; how they will be handled no one could say with certainty. Nevertheless, there are two areas where predictions are possible. First, we can say that a few changes will *not* happen, no matter how widely predicted they are today. Second, we can identify the needs, and with them the problems, that will challenge conventional wisdom and demand new and difficult decisions.

We find ourselves today—or so we are told—in a "revolt

against authority." Public belief and trust in all our institutions has dropped to the vanishing point; "bigness" is out, and "small is beautiful." It is claimed that we could and should disband the big organization. That management, whether in government or in business, is on the way out—or should be. And that we need to abjure the dangerous addiction to technology. None of these is likely to happen, I am afraid.

It is most unlikely that American society will, during the next ten years, slough off her big organizations and return to a non-institutional society, a society of small local communities and small units. This does not mean that there will be no need or opportunity to make our big institutions more effective or more responsive. It does not mean, above all, that there is no need for cutting back excess size and excess weight, both in government and in business institutions. The "conglomerate" we now know—and should have known all along—is counter-productive, whether it be a business conglomerate or that super-conglomerate, the Health, Education and Welfare Department (HEW) of the U.S. government. There are a great many institutions around that are too big, too fat, too diffuse to perform: businesses, hospitals, universities, and, above all, governmental units (e.g., Los Angeles County) or government agencies. We need a good deal of pruning, a good deal of dividing, a good deal of genuine autonomy and decentralization. But "small is better" is of course as meaningless as "big is better." Function decides size. And in order to function, pension fund socialism will need a good many big (some very big) organizations, as organs of economic production and distribution, as financial centers, and in government.

There is also no doubt that management will continue as a central organ and social function. American pension fund socialism explodes the old myth that "management"—or rather, modern organization—is the result of the "system." In its present-day form, one might call this the Marcuse myth.*

Large organizations, so runs the argument, are the result of "capitalism" and altogether of the "system." Change the system, and "organization" will disappear. This romantic illusion probably never had a great many adherents, though they always tended to make up by their noise level for what they lacked in numbers.

That the modern society of organizations presents problems is indeed obvious. But it should also be clear, from the experience of the United States in the last twenty-five years, that a society of organizations is not the result of the "system" and will not "wither away" under socialism any more than, as Marx had promised, the state "withers away" under socialism. In a society in which the performance of all major social tasks is entrusted to large institutions, management becomes, of necessity, the central organ and the central social function. Indeed, the society of pension fund socialism is more dependent than any other on management, its competence and its performance. Finally, we will not become less dependent on technology but, predictably, more dependent on it.

More important than the things that will not happen, however, are the new needs and demands. They have been neglected so far, primarily as a result of our failure to perceive the structural and demographic changes of pension fund socialism. But these, rather than the much-publicized and discussed things that won't happen, are what will

---

*Though it antedates Herbert Marcuse by at least seventy-five years and probably goes back to Walther Rathenau, the German industrialist-sociologist-politician slain by the Nazis in 1922, whose books, written before and during World War I, were the first attempt to come to grips with managerial society.

determine the issues of the years ahead. They require thought and understanding. They require changes in perception and attitude on the part of policy-makers and public opinion alike. They require hard decisions and hard work.

First will come the major economic needs, caused primarily by the shift in demographics. There will be a need for greater productivity of all wealth-producing resources. There will equally be a major need for proper management in order to ensure genuine economic growth of considerable proportions, growth which is neither "fat" nor inflation, but true growth in economic capacity, output, and performance.

Pension fund socialism secondly demands considerable attention to the area of industrial relations and to managing people at work. We can no longer expect the "system" —whatever it might be—to take care of the relationships between worker, work group, task, and management. And we can no longer postpone coming to grips with this problem.

The emergence of pension fund socialism also puts into question the traditional role and function of the labor union. Indeed, it can be said that the labor union will have to change its role, its function, and its fundamental approach, if it wants to survive as a viable institution. So far, however, no one can say what these changes should be, let alone whether they can be accomplished and how.

Further, pension fund socialism has created an entirely new form of "property," the pension claim. Increasingly, this property will control or at least own the major "productive resources" of society. Yet it is a very different form of property from those with which law and political theory have concerned themselves in the past.

Finally, pension fund socialism and the demographic

changes in the developed and the developing countries will have great impact on America's position and role in the world, and especially on the relationship between an America of pension fund socialism and the less developed countries of the Third World.

All these new needs will put heavy demands on our major institutions and their managements, with the pressure perhaps greatest on governments, particularly local governments. They will also require new, quite radical thinking and theory in both economics and politics.

The Demands on Economic Performance

Over the next ten years, until the mid- or late eighties, all key resources of production are likely to be in short supply unless there is prolonged worldwide depression. The work force will increase by only one-tenth, perhaps even less. Capital will be short, if only because an increasing portion of personal savings will become "pseudo-savings," the transfer payments that must support the rapidly growing number of older people past working age. And while no physical resource, except maybe food, will actually be in short supply in the world—even energy supplies are in fact abundant—the cost of physical resources, particularly the resources of energy, clean air, and usable water, are likely to go up or at least remain high.

At the same time, total production of goods and services will have to increase sharply or the standard of living is bound to fall. Where it now takes three and a half to four people in the labor force to support one person beyond retirement age, the dependency ratio will go up to two and a third to one within the next ten years—an increase of one-quarter. After that, the total population to be supported will still go up, albeit at a sharply reduced rate. Unless, therefore, the productivity of *all* key resources—human resources, capital and key physical resources—increases, real incomes and standards of living are bound to suffer. Productivity, to which in the twenty-five years since World War II we have paid very little attention, will become central. It will again be remembered that management—whether of business enterprise or of public-service institution—is paid, above all, to manage the productivity of key resources.

Capital is likely to be in even shorter supply than human resources. Productivity of capital will, therefore, have to increase faster than the productivity of human resources. But to increase human productivity at work will present new and, in many ways, more difficult challenges. In the first place, the composition of the labor force is changing rapidly. Where productivity of human resources traditionally meant the productivity of manual labor, it will increasingly mean the productivity of the knowledge worker, the man or woman who puts to work not brawn or manual skill but his knowledge—whether technical, professional, managerial, or administrative.

Among the older workers now retired or nearing retirement age, manual workers still predominate. But among young people now entering the labor force—those who constitute one of the new centers of demographic gravity—they are a minority. In 1975, manufacturing employment, using largely manual workers, still accounted for 23 percent of the American labor force. Another 4 percent worked on the farm; and another 16 percent was in blue-collar work in mining, transportation, or services (e.g., the telephone lineman). Manual workers thus came in 1976 to about 45 percent of the total labor force. Knowledge workers—technical, professional, managerial, and administrative personnel—came to 25 to 30 percent of the labor force, more than the total manufacturing employment. Sales personnel and clerical workers accounted for the rest, about one-quarter of the total.

By 1985, manufacturing employment is likely to have shrunk sharply; it will at most be 15 percent of the American labor force. Total manual employment is likely to be no more than one-third of the labor force. With sales and clerical jobs probably growing only moderately, the great increase will be in "knowledge" jobs which, in ten years, are likely to account for one-third or more of all jobs and for most of the new jobs.

Yet little work has been done on the productivity of the so-called knowledge worker. And there is little reason to believe that his productivity has increased much during the last seventy-five years. The teacher today, the researcher, the manager, is unlikely to be more productive than his or her predecessor was two generations back.

There has also been a shift in the place of employment. When we speak of productivity, we usually think of people in private employment—business or farming. But a full fifth of the labor force is employed by governments; and a very large group is employed by "public-service" institutions which, while not governments, are also not businesses —the hospital, for instance, or the university. Whether these workers are clerks or knowledge workers, they are normally not blue-collar manual workers. And by and large very little attention has been paid to the productivity of work and workers in the non-business, public-service institution. It is unlikely, however, that the situation has improved under benign neglect—though one hopes that the visible deterioration of the productivity of the postal system in all developed countries is the extreme exception rather than the rule. In fact, the productivity of the knowledge worker represents a major opportunity, since it is an axiom of productivity theory that the greatest gains are obtained by increasing the productivity of the most neglected resource. If the knowledge worker's productivity does not increase, then productivity cannot go up—though costs will. But if his or her productivity increases fast, total productivity will rise fast.

Knowledge work is work. The principles that apply to making manual work productive also apply to knowledge work. The most important of them is that increased productivity does not result from working harder, it results from "working smarter." The specific steps to be taken to obtain productivity and to increase it are also largely the same for knowledge work and manual work.* The first, crucial step is to select the right goals and to define the desired results. Next comes the selection of priorities and the concentration of human resources on those priorities. This is followed by an analysis of the tasks and their organization, which includes providing the worker, whether ditchdigger or physician, with the tools and information he needs. Then the worker has to be provided with the "feedback" from results to ensure that he or she knows whether the desired results have been obtained. Finally, those activities, products, or services which are no longer appropriate, have proven unable to produce results, or have outlived their usefulness† must be systematically abandoned.

The major difference between manual work and knowledge work is that in manual work we have tended to take for granted the selection of goals, the setting of priorities, the measurement of results and "feedback," and the orga-

---

*On productivity, see the section entitled "Productive Work and Achieving Worker" (Chapters 15–23) in *Management: Tasks, Responsibilities, Practices.*

†The only area of work to which these rules for productivity may not apply is the creation of new knowledge or new perception, that is, the work of the "pure" scientist or of the artist.

nized rejection of the outworn or unproductive. Therefore, we have focused on only one of the major steps in managing productivity: analyzing and organizing the task itself. This was largely a misunderstanding. The choice of what products to make is surely as important in manual work as in knowledge work. And the neglect of this decision is as likely to produce low productivity or no productivity at all in manual work as in knowledge work. Productivity does not mean the worker being more productive; it is management that has to "work smarter" to obtain productivity. But in manual work this tended to be overlooked.

In knowledge work, on the other hand, the decisions on goals, priorities, and abandonment are clearly the central factors. At the same time, these decisions require the active and responsible participation of the knowledge worker and his understanding. Managing a knowledge work force therefore demands a very different approach to the human resource on the part of all managements, whether profit-making businesses or governmental agencies. It also requires new information. At present, very few managements have much information on productivity. It is not that the figures are difficult to obtain, but they are not being produced routinely by the standard accounting model on which management information tends to be exclusively based. At least we know by and large what needs to be done, and how.

A hundred years ago, Karl Marx based his prediction of the inevitable and imminent collapse of what we now call "capitalism" or the "free-enterprise system" (both terms were, of course, not coined until after Marx's death) on the "law" of the diminishing productivity of capital.

What has happened instead is that for a century after the 1860s the productivity of capital in the developed countries —or rather, in developed countries with a market economy

—kept going up, except during the most severe depression years. This was one of the major achievements of modern business and the one on which all the other achievements of modern society perhaps rest in the last analysis. The achievement was in part entrepreneurial: a result of the steady shifting of capital from old and rapidly less productive areas of investment into the new, more highly productive areas of technical or social innovation which, as Joseph Schumpeter convincingly demonstrated sixty years ago, are the true "free capital" of a modern economy.

But the steady increase in the productivity of capital is equally the result of managerial action, of the continuing effort to increase the amount of productive work a given unit of capital performs in the economy. One example is commercial banking, where a single unit of capital today finances five times as large a volume of transactions as it did in Marx's time.

Yet Marx's basic logic was impeccable. If indeed the productivity of capital were to decline inexorably, a system based on market allocation of capital—that is, the system on which pension fund socialism bases itself—could not survive for more than a few short, crisis-ridden decades. Indeed, productivity of capital has been the one area in which the free-enterprise, market-based economics have shown decisive, in fact overwhelming, superiority over state-controlled "planned" economies. According to such figures as are available, the same increment of capital investment produces five to eight times as much additional output in a free-enterprise, market-based economy as it does in the Soviet Union or the Soviet Union's European satellites. Such low productivity of capital is inherent in "central planning," which can be defined as a system in which control—or the appearance of control—is being paid for by incurably low productivity of capital.

But productivity of capital in the free-enterprise, market-based economy has also been going down these last ten or fifteen years—though probably less so than in the centrally planned Communist economies. One reason is surely the rapid growth of the public sector, for governmental activities are characterized by very low productivity of capital and, as a rule, by total neglect of the management of capital. Another reason is that we have "underfunded" our capital requirements. In both energy and the environment we have postponed capital investment; now these capital deficits of the past will have to be made up, without obtaining increased production from the investments that represent the capital deficits of yesterday. Furthermore, in the quarter century after World War II, few businesses felt the need to manage capital productivity. Capital was plentiful and, on the whole, quite cheap. Just as few businesses managed for the productivity of energy, since energy appeared to be plentiful and very cheap, so few managements found it necessary to give more than routine attention to the productivity of capital. Indeed, very few business managements even had the information necessary to manage capital productivity. Again, the figures are not hard to obtain, but they are not routinely produced by the accounting system. Hence they are not, as a rule, produced at all.

This situation is already changing drastically as a result of the so-called liquidity crunch and the high cost of money during the last few years.* What few managements realize, however, is that the liquidity crunch and the cost of money are likely to be with us for a long time. Very few have yet grasped that the main causes are not the energy crisis, the stock market, the recession, nor even high capital demand.

---

*A short discussion of what is needed to manage the productivity of capital can be found in an article of mine, "Managing Capital Productivity," in *The Wall Street Journal,* July 24, 1975.

Rather, the main causes are the demographic shift and the diversion of yesterday's traditional capital flow into "transfer payments" to support the rapidly growing older population. And this shift will continue. Even if we succeed in raising the rate of capital formation and in designing new channels of capital allocation and distribution (the problems discussed in the preceding section of this book), capital is likely to remain scarce and expensive.

This means, in the first place, that liquidity, cash flow, and financial structure will again become central to business and business management. In the last twenty-five years, they could be considered secondary, with volume of sales and profit-and-loss statements being primary. Now financial structure, financial supply, and the use of available funds—the traditional, even old-fashioned concerns—will again move into the center of the stage and demand utmost management attention and skill.

Secondly, managements will have to organize themselves for continued, systematic work on the productivity of capital. To finance the volume of production and distribution that the demographic changes require, managements may well have to double within the next ten years or so the productivity of capital employed in the business, whether the money be equity, debt capital, retained earnings, or what-have-you. This can be accomplished precisely because capital management has widely been neglected. Some of the leaders in this field (in the United States, General Electric may be one illustration) have been managing capital all along at a rate of productivity substantially higher than those of companies in comparable industries which are considered and consider themselves to be well managed. But it requires hard and systematic work.

Traditionally, productivity has been managed by "trade-offs" between various factors of productivity. The traditional, and indeed the easy, way to raise the productivity of labor was to increase capital investment; or, higher labor productivity could be traded off against lower productivity of physical resources. (This is one of the main reasons for the rapid rise in energy consumption during the last fifteen years, in which greater energy input per unit of output was used to decrease labor input per unit of output.)

Such a "trade-off" between the productivity of various factors of production will no longer be possible; at the least it will not give much increased productivity. Economists classify industries as "labor-intensive," "capital-intensive," or "raw material-intensive"; this then determines what "trade-offs" are most likely to bring about an increase in overall productivity. But increasingly all businesses, all industries, and all public-service institutions will be "labor-intensive" *and* "capital-intensive" *and* "materials-intensive." None of them will be able to increase total productivity through a "trade-off" which sacrifices the productivity of one key resource to obtain higher productivity for another. All productive resources will therefore have to be managed for increased productivity. This, perhaps more than the demand of productivity for the human resource or for capital, is the true "innovation" in management ahead of us. Few managements, whether of businesses or of public-service institutions, have yet faced up to it.

One of the significant political innovations of the last decade has been the "environmental impact statement" which now has to accompany the capital-spending proposals and policies of both businesses and governments. We will have to develop a parallel "productivity impact statement" in business and public-service institutions alike. For productivity is also an "environment," also man-made or man-unmade, also "endangered"—and equally important for the welfare and survival of the human species.

Businesses have always known that managements are paid to make resources productive, though they have not always acted on their knowledge. For business managements, therefore, the new demands—to manage knowledge work and knowledge workers for productivity, and money and capital for productivity—will mean only that they have to do better, far better, what they supposedly do already. But for the public-service institution, and especially for governmental agencies and units, these are *new* demands. And they are demands at odds with the ethos, the vision, the traditions, and the practices of such institutions.* Public-service institutions, and again especially governmental agencies, operate on a "budget" rather than on the basis of results obtained against performance. There is no incentive for productivity, and indeed not even for efficiency, in the budget-based institution. Lower costs, in effect, tend to penalize the budget-based institution rather than reward it. Furthermore, public-service institutions find it hard to define goals and almost impossible to define priorities. Finally, for a public-service institution, particularly a governmental agency, to abandon the obsolete, the unsuccessful, the unproductive activity or service, is the most difficult decision of all. It is always "controversial." Yet this is the absolute prerequisite to productivity, especially the productivity of knowledge work and knowledge worker.

The demand to manage the productivity of capital is likewise going to be a shock to the public-service institution. Governments do not even think in terms of "capital," let alone attempt to manage it. Nor have public-service institutions, especially governments, concerned them-

*On the fundamental characteristics of the public-service institution, see the section on "Performance in the Service Institution" (Chapters 11–14) in *Management: Tasks, Responsibilities, Practices*.

selves much with liquidity and cash flow, financial structure and the allocation of money. The budget shows where the money goes, but it does not show why or with what efficiency or effectiveness. In the next ten years public-service institutions, and above all local governments, can expect to find themselves under both increasing and conflicting pressures. The demand for performance and productivity is already sharply on the rise. It is bound to become more strident as the rising number of older dependents puts pressure on incomes and living standards. And the fact that the greatest problem for state and local governments is to fund their pension obligations will only make the pressure even greater. At the same time, local governments will find themselves under equal pressure to maintain the traditions of the political process, which presupposes subordinating performance and productivity to consensus and to the striving for compromise rather than decision. But there are "right" and "wrong" compromises, depending not upon political acceptability but on the objective specifications of the situation which a given decision has to satisfy.

Altogether, productivity contradicts the essence of the political process. For productivity demands priorities and concentration. It demands willingness and ability to abandon. The political process, on the other hand, always aims at consensus rather than decision, at continuing yesterday rather than sloughing it off. It used to be said—and it is still widely believed—that this is characteristic of the political process in a democracy. We now know all too well that the "political process" in the most absolute dictatorship does not operate any differently.*

*On this, we have an enormous amount of information in respect to the decisionmaking process in Hitler's Germany, where decisions were actually far more likely to be lost to pressures, lobbying, and wrong compromise than under democratic governments in wartime Britain or in wartime U.S.A. The same subordination of decision to "politics," according to the available evidence, is true of Soviet Russia, both under Stalin and today.

Politics has been defined as the "art of the possible." Productivity is, in effect, the "art of the necessary." The need for productivity is therefore going to challenge the traditional, deeply embedded managerial practices and philosophies of the public-service institution and, above all, of the governmental agencies—with local governments probably the most seriously challenged. At the very least, a distinction must be made between those activities of public-service institutions that are "operational"—the police department, for instance, garbage disposal, but also the post office or housing finance—and the "policy-making" ones. The former needs to be "managed," and managed for performance and productivity rather than for consensus. The latter properly belong under the political process. No matter how well understood, this is very difficult to do, as the experience of Britain's nationalized industry shows. These industries—the coal mines, the railroads, the airlines, and so on—were set up to be operated for performance and productivity. But the crucial decisions have again and again been based on political expediency, on political pressures, and on the desire to obtain consensus or at least to placate pressure groups (and by no means only the trade unions). The problem of reconciling political process and social need remains unsolved.

Public-service institutions, with local governments in the lead, can therefore expect a turbulent period during which the fundamentals of governance will be challenged. The next ten years are likely to be as active a period of local government reform, local government innovation, and local government policy as was the opening decade of the twentieth century for the United States—or as, fifty years earlier, the mid-nineteenth-century years were for most European countries.

The demand for productivity also creates a need for a shift in economic theory. Economic theory (as has been said for over 100 years) has been following the development of physics in its structure and paradigms.* It is true that economics in the early nineteenth century did adopt the basic approach of Newtonian physics, then a century old. The father of modern economics, David Ricardo, quite consciously based his approach on a Newtonian universe and on Newtonian concepts of mechanics. But the age of "macro-physics" came to an end early in this century with the discovery of radioactivity, of the quantum, and of relativity. The universe of the modern physicist is a micro-universe, his model the world of atoms, atomic particles, and the forces between atomic and sub-atomic phenomena. Economic theory, however, for the same seventy-five years, has become more and more a theory of the macro-economy. Nineteenth-century economists still concerned themselves with events in the individual business, with decisions on the part of individual businessmen, individual consumers, individual savers. Above all, they were still preoccupied with productivity. The modern economist, beginning with the monetary economists before Keynes, has brushed aside concern with the micro-economy. His model treats the micro-economy the way Newtonian physicists treated molecules and atoms, i.e., as statistical, determined by events, in themselves without significance and without impact on the system. Whether the modern economist is a fiscal economist (a Keynesian) or a monetary economist (a post-Keynesian) does not matter. His model is a model of the "national" economy, that is, essentially a model of governmental decisions. Micro-phenomena—and that means productivity, capital investment, or allocation of resources —are assumed to be determined by macro-economic events, that is, by governmental policy. Even as a macro-

*This idea goes back to the distinguished mid-Victorian English economist and social critic, Walter Bagehot.

economic model this no longer works. The world economy, as already said, has proven to be the only true "macro-economy." But the economist may also have to shift radically to a micro-model, like the physicist seventy-five years ago, and to a theory based on micro-economics and above all on productivity.

The demand for productivity which pension fund socialism with its demographics creates therefore also implies a demand for a new economic theory—new not only in its answers but in its assumptions, concerns, and approaches: its questions.

The Need for Growth Management

It is fashionable these days to preach and to predict "zero growth." But zero growth is unlikely, and would in fact be a catastrophe were it to happen.

Every 50 or 60 years, these past 250 years, there has been a decade in which businessmen, politicians, and economists in the world economy's "developed countries" expected speculative growth to go on forever at an exponential rate: between 1710 and 1720, the years of the "South Sea Bubble," the Dutch tulip craze, and John Law's monumental swindle in France; around 1770; after 1830; around 1870, in the years in which most of what passes for "modern industry" was born; and around 1910 (aborted in Europe by World War I, but continuing in the U.S. until 1929). The 1960s, in other words, were just a "re-run" of the same "go-go decade" which has punctuated modern economic development for more than two centuries.

Every "go-go decade" believed that there were no limits to growth. And every one ended in débacle, leaving behind a massive hangover. After every "go-go decade," prophecies of zero growth become popular again. But except for the years between World War I and World War II, vigorous economic growth always either continued or was resumed very soon after the "go-go decade" had come to an end. However, the aftermath of a "go-go decade" always does bring substantial structural changes in the economy. Economic growth always changes and shifts to new foundations. What was "smart management" during the "go-go decade" rapidly becomes inappropriate, if not actually incompetent.

It is not impossible that the developed countries and, above all, the United States do face a "zero growth" period today. But if so it would be unnecessary, the result of incompetence rather than of economics. The demands are there; indeed, they are very great. And the resources to satisfy them exist.

More important, however, growth—and growth of very substantial proportions—is a major priority caused by the demographic shifts. Only with very substantial growth can the economic demands of the population change and very large numbers of "dependents" be satisfied. That such growth will be different from the growth of the last thirty years is practically certain. It will (as already stressed several times) have to be primarily based on capital investment rather than on consumption. But it will have to be substantial growth. In fact, the growth rate needed by the United States just to maintain the real income and standards of living of a population in which the older people past working age are one of the centers of demographic gravity is higher than the growth rate during most of the years between the end of World War II and the early seventies. But it will have to be managed growth.

Every business, therefore, will require a growth policy. Businesses must first know how much growth they need. In a developing market, a business has to grow sufficiently to avoid becoming marginal; it has to have enough leadership position in its market not to be rapidly squeezed out as soon as a minor setback forces the retailer to cut down the number of items he stocks to the three or four fast-moving brands.

Far more important is the need to distinguish between desirable and undesirable growth. For a twelve-year-old to grow 6 inches in a year is healthy growth, bone and muscle. But for the forty-year-old man to put on 20 pounds is not desirable growth, it is "fat." A certain amount of fat is, of course, necessary; beyond the minimum, however, fat becomes a burden on the system and even endangers it. Cancer is also growth, very fast growth. An institution needs to be able to manage its growth so that it represents strength. It has to be able to control fat. It has to be able to spot cancer early and to eliminate it by radical surgery.

The rules are simple. Growth that results in increased productivity of the combined resources of production (human resources, capital and physical resources) is bone and muscle. Growth that does not result in increased productivity of the resources but only in more assets, a bigger budget; a larger staff, or more sales volume—most of the growth, in other words, of the "conglomerates" during the "go-go decade" of the sixties—is fat. Up to a point the "fat" will support healthy tissue. It may support more research, for instance; or it can make possible a capital investment in equipment to protect the environment which otherwise could not be made. But beyond a fairly low point, "fat" is a burden and needs to be controlled. And growth which actually damages the productivity of key resources is a cancer requiring drastic surgery.

But while the rules are simple, few managements know them and even fewer apply them. In the period ahead, in which both an increase in real productivity and a genuine growth will be necessary, managing growth will become a central challenge for business and a severe test of managerial competence.

Public-service institutions, too, will have to learn to manage growth. Both the American hospital and the American university have been through an era even giddier than the "go-go era" of the conglomerates in business. In both, much of the growth has been fat rather than bone and muscle, and some has undoubtedly been cancer. At the same time these institutions have no direct market test—though they are increasingly coming under competitive pressures. They therefore need all the more to manage growth and to control it. The same is true of the governmental institutions. There the rule should be that growth of budget is undesirable and indeed *lowers* the performance capacity of the institution unless it results in higher productivity of all resources measured against specific, clear goals. Otherwise, growth in a purely budget-based institution is almost certain to mean diffusion of energies and efforts rather than an expansion in capacity and performance.

Work and Worker: The Social Demands

When Charles Wilson of GM proposed the first of the "modern" pension plans, twenty-six years ago, he expected it to have profound impact on industrial relations as well as on human relations. It was this prospect that persuaded a skeptical General Motors board to accept his proposal. The general public shared these expectations; so did the labor union leadership when it first resisted the plan.

The employees have, indeed, through the pension fund, become the principal owners of America's businesses. In fact, they own a much larger share than Charles Wilson ever expected them to. Yet nothing has happened to either work or the worker. The relationships at work between worker, work group, task, and boss have not been affected at all. And this could have been predicted; in fact, it was by a good many people.

Those who propose today that we invent the pension plan all over again—Louis Kelso in this country or Ota Šik in Europe—are even more sanguine than Charles Wilson was. They promise that an industrial utopia will result from tying business performance to the employee's financial security through pension plans investing in company stock. Ota Šik, for instance, pushes his plan with the promise that it will overcome the "conflict between wage fund and capital fund" and, with it, industrial warfare. But one can say dogmatically that such plans will have just as little impact on work and worker as American pension fund socialism has had.

For well over a century, if not for longer, there has been a persistent belief that a change in the "system" which made the workers the "owners" would automatically take care of the problems of industrial society, whether the disease be diagnosed as "alienation," as "subordination of man to the machine," as "the assembly line," "exploitation," or simply the boredom and drudgery of work. But for well over 100 years we have also known that this belief is a delusion. For worker ownership has a much longer history than most people realize. It has been tried many times, and has never had any but the most transitory impact on the work, the worker, or the relationships at work. Even total ownership of a business and full worker control seem to have little effect on industrial and human relations at work.

One example—an American one—was the Hershey

Chocolate Company, totally owned by and for the benefit of the employees, which then exploded into one of the most bitter strikes in American labor history. Another example is the German optical company Zeiss, which was given to the employees in 1906 without any great impact, if any, on industrial and human relations in the company. Today, outside the United States, the same absence of results is reported from Yugoslavia, where the workers both "own" and "control" the country's larger businesses.

An identical lesson has been taught during the same period by the other, much more widely publicized change in the "system": nationalization. The worst industrial relations in Great Britain today are in some of the nationalized industries, especially coal mining and the railroads. The worst industrial relations in France are at Renault, the nationalized automobile company. And the worst industrial relations in Japan are on the Japanese National Railways.

But the most massive experience is certainly the American experiment of the last twenty-five years. This should once and for all explode the myth which sees the key to "industrial warfare" or "alienation" as lying in "ownership" or any other facet of the "system."

One reason is a simple economic one: no matter how lush the profits of a business, the employees' primary interest must be in the income from their job. Business profit in the economy, even in good years, rarely runs to more than one-tenth of income from wages and salaries. Hence the job, even in terms of its economic benefits alone, is quite properly ten times as important to the employee as sharing the profits or sharing ownership.

Even more important than economics are the psychological, human, and power relationships which are determined on the job rather than outside it. These are the relationships between worker, work group, task, immediate boss, and management;* "human relations" means exactly that: human relations. Just as good and bad marriages are not made by the Civil Code, so good or bad work relationships are not made by the "system."

There is indeed abundant evidence that "industrial relations" are not a matter of the "industrial system" but pertain to wherever people work together in an organization. There is no evidence at all for the romantic illusion that the pre-industrial workers, whether craftsmen, journeymen, or hired farm hands, loved their work, loved their masters, and lived in harmony with themselves, their tasks, their fellow employees, and their employers. The difference is not "capitalism," the "machine," or the "assembly line." The difference is simply that in pre-industrial societies most people did not work in organizations. What we term "industrial relations" or "human relations" are the relationships that characterize work and the worker in organizations.

The "system" can indeed make decent human relations impossible. Slavery, for instance, debases both master and slave. But good human relations can only be made where the relationships function, at the place of work and on the job. Just as the "system" cannot be blamed for the problems of industrial and human relations at work, so "human nature" does not explain or excuse them. Human nature wants, expects, indeed, demands respect for work and task,

*This was first spelled out and documented in my two books, *Concept of the Corporation* (New York: John Day, 1946) and *The New Society* (New York: Harper & Row, 1950). Since then, Frederick Herzberg, formerly at Case Western Reserve and now at the University of Utah, has provided a wealth of experimental support, as have a good many other industrial psychologists and sociologists. Particularly valuable are the Glacier Mental Studies undertaken in the fifties and sixties in England by the psychologist Elliot Jacques and the industrialist Lord Wilfred Brown. The whole subject is discussed, with many examples, in the section "Making Work Productive and the Worker Achieving," in *Management: Tasks, Responsibilities, Practices.*

and achievement in both. In every survey the overwhelming majority of people at work stress the positive aspects of their job and try to gloss over the negative ones. They do not expect "happiness"; they expect achievement, responsibility, and performance.

And that too we have known for 150 years. In the 1820s Robert Owen (1771–1858) took over a bankrupt cotton mill in Lanark, Scotland, and turned it within a few years into a thriving business. Owen did not put in capital; he was almost penniless himself. He was no financial wizard, knew nothing about technology, and had never heard of "marketing." All he did was to manage the work so that tasks were clear and standards high, and to allow the worker— indeed, to demand from him or her—a high degree of responsibility for job, work group, and performance.

Owen's approach has been tried many times since, always with the same success. His most faithful imitator was Alfried Krupp. The emergence of Krupp to dominance in Europe's heavy industry was largely the result of his application of Owen's principle of industrial and human relations; so was its ability to rise twice out of the ashes of a lost war because of the loyalty of the workers, the "Kruppianers," to the firm. Today Owen's principles underlie to a considerable extent IBM's rise to dominance in the world's computer industry. The application of the same approach in the form of "continuous learning" (i.e., organized individual and work group responsibility for task, work group organization, and performance) is a main secret behind the "Japanese miracle" of the last twenty-five years. And in Great Britain, two Quaker industrialists, Cadbury and Rowntree, applied Owen's principles to become for many decades world leaders in the chocolate industry.

The legendary production performance of American and British industry in World War II likewise rested largely on making the worker primarily responsible for his own job, for his group, for learning, and for performance. Every single one of the "innovations" that are publicized today— "job enrichment," the restructuring of the traditional automobile assembly line at Chrysler or at Volvo, or group responsibility for job design, safety, and workloads—was first practiced successfully a century ago and has been rediscovered successfully many times since.

The question why these lessons have not been learned (or when learned, as in U.S. and British industry in World War II, were forgotten so fast) goes well beyond the scope of this book. One reason was surely the obsession with "macro-phenomena" and "systems" which characterized what the eighteenth and nineteenth centuries called "rationalism." Industrial relations, however, are clearly micro-phenomena. The "industrial system" is made up of a multitude of specific relationships and experiences at the "molecular" level: the individual task, the specific job, and a concrete, personal set of human relationships. And this went against the period's conventional wisdom and its world view, whether that of Karl Marx, of the "capitalists," or of the sociological theoreticians of right or left. The success stories, beginning with Owen, were always widely publicized; Owen's Lanark was a "must" for the European traveler of the period and a major tourist attraction for years. But they were not copied by many.

To believe in the "system" as the answer was so comfortable and comforting. Instead of imitating Owen, the industrialists of the time expected "capitalism" to produce industrial harmony. Owen and Krupp were greatly admired by the German "Katheder Socialisten" (academic socialists) who dominated German social thinking between 1880 and World War I. But if "socialism" could be expected automatically to cure the problems of work and working, emulating Owen or Krupp must have seemed pointless. Surely, if changing the "system" will change industrial and human relations without any effort, there is no point in working hard at them in the meantime.

And it is hard work.* But work we can no longer avoid or postpone. The lesson of American pension fund socialism is surely decisive. No longer can any manager plead the *mañana* of a "change in the system" to escape his responsibility to manage work and to make the worker achieve. If socializing the productive resources of the world's leading industrial country does not change industrial and human relations at work, no other change in the "system" will. There is thus no longer any excuse for a management that does not tackle this task within its own institution, be it business, hospital, or government agency. And the job has by now been done often enough so that we know what to do and how.

Pension fund socialism will put tremendous pressures on managements—and, as the next section will discuss, on unions as well—to go to work on industrial, human, and work relations. Increased productivity, above all, demands a restructuring of industrial and human relations. The demographic change also makes work on industrial and human relations imperative. The knowledge worker, in particular, is not productive unless he is responsible for task, work group, and performance. He will not be productive unless industrial relations at the work place are put in order.

Under pension fund socialism, industrial relations thus emerge as a major priority and a major opportunity but, above all, as a major challenge to management. It is a challenge that confronts business management and the

*For a full discussion, see the section "Productive Work and Achieving Worker" (Chapters 15–23) in *Management: Tasks, Responsibilities, Practices.*

management of public-service and governmental organizations alike.

Can the Labor Union Survive Pension Fund Socialism?

Of all the institutions of industrial society, the labor union has had the most spectacular rise in this century. In the 1900s, the labor union was barely tolerated in most countries, and at best marginal. Today the labor union has become so powerful that in Great Britain the Trade Union Congress, though perhaps with considerable exaggeration, is often called the "real government." In the United States, the labor unions are surely the true "fourth branch" of government rather than the mass media or the bureaucracy. They occupy the same power position in every developed country except Communist Russia, where Stalin ruthlessly suppressed them around 1930.

The labor union serves a necessary function in a society of organizations. Any organization, whether business, university, government agency, or hospital, has to have a management. And management means power and control. The labor unions serve as the countervailing power. "Every action creates a reaction," says one of the fundamental laws of physics. The labor union is the "reaction" to management's "action." It is, therefore, not confined to capitalism, and certainly not to business. Indeed, unions are more needed and more powerful by now among employees of non-businesses, particularly government employees. And whenever a labor union itself becomes an employer, it soon finds that its employees organize themselves into a labor union against their trade union bosses.

The labor union has shown amazing resilience. Wherever a dictatorship in a developed country has come to an end, an effective trade union is the first institution to re-emerge. It happened in Germany after Hitler. As soon as Franco's régime in Spain showed the first signs of slackening in the late sixties, labor unions, though officially completely illegal, sprang up as the first effective opposition. It is a reasonable guess that independent labor unions would be among the first organizations of a post-totalitarian Russia.

Yet for all its visibility and power, its function and resilience, the labor union is uniquely vulnerable. It is an "opposition" which can never become the government. Its job is to oppose management, but it can never assume itself the management function. Wherever it does so, even to a limited extent, it rapidly loses its ability to discharge its main and necessary function—that of opposition. The union leaders who sit on the governing boards of Britain's nationalized industries, the Coal Board, for instance, or British Railways, have carefully limited their role to representing the employees against management. Still, they have lost, in large measure, control of the unions, which have shifted to the "militant" shop stewards who oppose union leadership as vigorously as they oppose management.

Above all, the labor union, despite its power and visibility, is a derivative institution. We cannot get rid of management and the management function as long as our society remains one of institutions. A change of system may lead to a change of the people who do the managing and occupy managing positions. It may lead to a change of titles. And the managers may have new and different bosses to answer to. But it does not change the need for managements nor, in essentials, what managing means and what managers do. It does not even change the power of managers and management to any significant degree.

Yet management can function very well without a labor union. Indeed most managers, whether in government or private enterprise, are convinced that they could manage much better without the union. Hitler could abolish the world's oldest, most respected and strongest union movement—the German labor unions—by sending a lieutenant and ten men to occupy trade union headquarters. And until Hitler was overthrown by foreign armies, there was not even an underground labor movement in Nazi Germany. Labor leaders are acutely sensitive to their vulnerability. Despite all their power, they see themselves as threatened, besieged, weak. To the outsider, their patent insecurity is often a puzzle. But labor union leaders know that their power depends on society's sufferance.

Pension fund socialism threatens to bring this vulnerability of the labor union into the open. Whatever the role of the labor union under pension fund socialism, it has to decide among equally dangerous alternatives, each challenging its cohesion.

The employees—the people whose organization the labor union asserts itself to be and whom it claims to represent—are now increasingly both "employees" and "owners." Increasingly, they have an interest both in their job and its wage or salary, and an interest both in the performance and the profitability of enterprise. And increasingly, they stand in two relationships to the "system," which according to union logic and union rhetoric are mutually exclusive.

The labor movement can choose to ignore pension fund socialism. This would be the normal reaction for an American union leader—who does not challenge the "system" as such, but demands that one interest in it, that of the employee as employee, be given pride of place. It was an American unionist, Victor Reuther of the United Automo-

bile Workers, who invented "co-determination" when serving in the American Military Occupation of Germany after
World War II. Under "co-determination" union representatives sit on the supervisory boards of businesses,
though they are not, under Germany's corporation law,
part of management, which is a separate body. But no other
American union leader has had much use for "co-determination" so far. Not one of them has yet wanted any part of
the management task, whether through "co-determination" or "co-responsibility." To ignore the emergence of
pension fund socialism, if not to deny that it has come into
being, is thus the almost instinctive first reaction of the
American labor leader.

The second alternative for labor is to try to use pension
fund socialism as a means to expand union power by
becoming the representative of the employees in their role
as principal owners. This will increasingly become more
attractive to the union leader the more visible pension fund
socialism becomes. For the union leader will, quite cor-
rectly, point out that the employees deserve to occupy the
traditional ownership position of control over management, or at least a share in such control. And the fact that
in Europe—particularly Northern Europe—"worker participation on the board" is rapidly becoming commonplace
and established by law, will provide a telling argument. It
should also make the argument a very attractive one to the
American liberal, to the mass media, and to the academi-
cian.

Both alternatives are however fraught with grave risk for
the American trade union. To ignore pension fund socialism can only aggravate the already existing threat to the
cohesion of the union: the tug of war between the younger
workers and the older members, between those whose
main interest is in the size of the weekly cash wage and

those who are increasingly interested in their future pension rights. In the New York City crisis, many of the older employees—teachers, policemen, firemen—would have preferred even severe cuts in City employment and expenditures to bailing out the City through the investment of pension fund assets in City bonds of dubious value. Such cuts would not have been a great threat to the older people with seniority rights, whereas misinvestment of pension fund assets surely is. This conflict was kept from exploding only by the great personal authority of some of the City employees' leaders. But every labor leader knows that the conflict exists and that it threatens the cohesion of his union as well as his hold on his job.

The more the center of gravity in the labor force shifts from blue-collar worker to knowledge worker, the riskier it will be to ignore the emergence of pension fund socialism. Knowledge workers are not more intelligent than blue-collar workers, but they do have a wider horizon, know more, are better informed. They are also, in very large numbers, fairly sophisticated (or at least fairly active) investors. The blue-collar worker, the "man on the assembly line," knows that he has a pension coming to him; but he may never have heard of a pension fund, let alone of the way it is invested. The engineer, or the accountant, however, knows very well and is vitally interested. Such men are themselves in the habit of managing or mismanaging investments. To be sure, the job is still the center of their interest and their first concern. But the older they get, and the more their concern for the pension grows, the more interest they take in the funds that manage their pension assets, and the more aware they are likely to be that their pension depends on their ownership stake in American business.

If American labor chooses to ignore the emergence of

144 · *The Pension Fund Revolution*

pension fund socialism, it runs therefore the one risk no trade union can possibly afford: the risk of a competing organization's claiming to represent the employee. For if the union does not assume responsibility for the employee as owner, some other organization will do so sooner or later. Such an organization might take half a dozen different forms, but in any form it would be a competitor to the labor union. It would be an organization of "labor"—not representing the employee as an employee against management, but ownership against management and employees alike. And this would deprive the union movement of its sole claim to legitimacy, power, and influence: the claim that it is the "voice of the employee." It is not mere rhetoric that makes the labor union leaders constantly talk of the "unity of labor." Their power, their claim to be heard and, to a large measure, their claim to the allegiance of the members, rests on their monopoly on employee representation.

The second alternative is equally risky: to accept pension fund socialism and to assert the labor union's role as representing the employee as owner. This would force the union leaders into taking the enterprise's, even management's, side against the employee. The interest of the employee as an owner is by no means identical, at least not in the short run, with the interest of the employee as an employee. To an "employee," "profits" are something that is being "taken away from the worker," always seen as enormous and surely "excessive." To an "owner," on the other hand, profits are absolutely necessary; they are, in effect, the foundation for his own future security. Instead of being excessive or exorbitant, they will almost always be seen as inadequate. To the employee, "productivity" is a dirty word (even where there are Joint Productivity Councils of management and labor, as in most British and some U.S.

industries—the steel industry, for example). To an owner, "productivity" is what he pays management for.

The American union leader who steadfastly refuses to become identified with "management" in any shape or form has abundant reason for his position. Only the most autocratic and powerful of American union leaders was able to do so and yet maintain his hold on his union: John L. Lewis who, in the 1940s, forced a ruthless cut in employment on his own membership and pushed for both higher productivity and higher company profits in order to save the American coal industry. He did save the industry and with it the jobs of those miners who remained employed. But after his death, the union collapsed—and has not yet recovered. Few union leaders have the authority and power that enabled John L. Lewis to act as both unchallenged union leader and "elder statesman" of the coal-mining industry.

Either alternative must therefore be equally unattractive to an intelligent labor union leader. In their public persona, union leaders in this country vehemently deny that there is a problem at all. But behind the closed doors of union headquarters, union leaders are worried—and their staff people, whose job it is to chart union policy, are worried a great deal more. For no clear, safe, attractive course of action is available, or at least visible so far.

Some things are becoming reasonably clear, though not for that reason any easier. It is, for instance, clear that it would be highly desirable, for the American labor movement, for the American economy, and for the pension funds, if labor came to be represented on the boards of both businesses and pension funds—but not necessarily through labor leaders themselves serving on the board. Rather, the "public" director—somebody independent, well known, with expertise and strong ties to both management and unions—might serve, perhaps with an express mandate to represent the country's employees in their capacity as the company's principal owners, and to be in close working contact with them and the unions that represent them. This might, of course, put the "public" or "professional" director in conflict with the union that represents the company's own employees. Yet he would still be an employee representative, still give the country's employees the voice, representation, and access they should have as owners. And he might provide the bridge to the new "owners" (the pension fund beneficiaries), which the enterprise and its management, but also its unions, need.

Above all, strong but independent employee representation is required on the governing boards of the pension funds. Both the present job and the future pension are employee interests. Both require guardianship for the employee through his representatives. But they are distinct interests and must be represented separately, otherwise the future will always be subordinated to the present. And as a good many American labor leaders learned from New York City, the integrity of the employee's pension fund assets (increasingly the employee's main asset, and his main resource next to his job) needs to be protected.

Similarly, the interest of the country's employees, in their capacity as owners, in productivity and performance must be represented. Unless productivity and performance improve, wages and pension claims cannot be maintained at their real value, which will either be cut openly or cut through inflation. Unions and union leaders know that they cannot afford to be blamed for inflation by the public or by their membership.

The labor union will somehow have to become an integrative force—without losing its function as the representative of the employee *qua* employee that acts to some degree as the "anti-force" to the power of management within the organization. This will surely require drastic changes in industrial relations and hard, sustained work at making the worker productive and responsible. It will require also an understanding on the part of the employee of his own dual role as employee within the organization and "owner" of the business. Here the shift in work-force structure to the knowledge worker should prove helpful. For the knowledge worker anyhow sees himself, as a rule, in a dual capacity; at once as an employee and a member of the managerial, decision-making groups.

Still, the trade union which pension fund socialism requires will be a very different trade union from that of the past or present. Of all our social institutions, none is as profoundly challenged in its function, its commitments, and its rhetoric.

The role and function of the trade union in society are becoming altogether problematical because of the very success of the labor movement. How much longer can any developed society afford the "right to strike"? How long can it afford wage dictation by union power? How long will it put up with jurisdictional demarcation lines and union restrictions on access to craft and work? And yet how can any trade union movement function if these powers are taken away or fettered? Yet ultimately the greatest problem of the American trade union may not be the scope and limitations of its traditional functions but the dilemmas of its new role under pension fund socialism.

The New Meaning of Property

Man has a right to property, said John Locke in his manifesto of liberal society, *The Second Treatise on Government,* 300 years ago, because he has "commingled his labor with it." Pension fund claims based on deferred wages and a reward for "labor" come closer to fitting Locke's explanation of property than almost any other form of wealth. Aside from this, the pension fund claim does not answer any definition of "property" we know. It cannot be divided, sold, mortgaged, borrowed against, lent, assigned, bequeathed, or inherited. Indeed, to call it a "claim" should make any lawyer raise his eyebrows. A "claim" implies a specific title and an ascertainable value. Even the rare pension claim which comes closest to meeting these specifications—the claim that is fully funded, fully vested, has death benefits, and a guaranteed contractual payout period—is both in title and value "contingent" rather than "certain" until the beneficiary has died, i.e., ceased to have a claim.

The word "property" has a nice solid ring to it. But no one would call the blue-collar worker enrolled in his company's pension plan a "man of property." Pension fund claims are pure abstractions. They are blips in a computer memory and hypothetical computations. This is hardly what "property" has always meant nor what it still means in common usage. But what is commonly called property increasingly has little or nothing to do with ownership of productive resources, except on the farm. It is "personal property": the house one owns, the furniture in it, the automobile, the TV set, and the kitchen appliances. These things cost money; they have resale value in varying degree. Yet they do not produce goods and services, that is, "wealth." Long ago Karl Marx pointed out the fundamental difference between property in wealth-producing resources, that is, in the "means of production," and personal property. Only the first, Marx said, has anything to do with the structure of economy and society. For only ownership of the "means of production" yields profit and power.

Personal property is irrelevant economically and socially. Only ownership of wealth-producing resources would be taken over by a Socialist society. Personal property would remain personal property. The Soviet citizen cannot own wealth-producing resources. But he can and does own personal property—a vacation home in the country, a car, or a phonograph—and can buy and sell these freely as long as he does not make a business out of buying and selling.

This is, of course, not egalitarianism. But Stalin was justified in invoking Marx when he condemned egalitarianism as anti-Marxist heresy. Or at least he was closer to the position of the master than Mao or the egalitarians of today's New Left. Personal property, provided only that it cannot be converted into ownership of productive resources, simply did not concern Marx very much one way or another.

Since Marx's day, personal property has diffused to the great masses. It has become "standard of living." And ownership of productive resources is fast becoming a pension claim—owned by the employees and the product of their "labor"—the reward for work rather than "surplus value," the product of "exploitation," or "rent." Pension claims increasingly hold controlling ownership in America's productive resources: her mills, mines, and machines; her banks and department stores; and, indeed, her main capital resources except farm land. It is the abstract, contingent pension claim that holds increasingly the traditional right of ownership to the "full enjoyment of the fruits of property."

It is also this intangible abstraction, this blip in a computer memory, this contingent claim of undefined and undefinable value, that is the main asset and the principal wealth of most American families.

It is quite unlikely that the pension claim will turn into

a tangible and fungible asset with ascertainable value, which can be bought and sold, pledged, lent, bequeathed and inherited, let alone into an asset that can be converted into direct personal ownership of the "means of production." To be sure, claims—to an office, to a stipend, or to a share in revenues—have again and again in history turned into property of the most tangible form in the course of a few generations. But it is the essence of a pension claim that it is tied to one person and frozen, without value, until this person either dies or lives to receive his pension. It is of its essence that it is contingent, based on probability assumptions rather than certainty. Yet the assets which underlie this claim, say shares of the General Electric Company in the portfolio of the pension fund, are definitely "titles of ownership" to "means of production" and have all the characteristics of property.

The emergence of pension fund socialism thus radically alters the meaning of "property." At the very least, it creates something new—call it an "asset"—which is more important for the majority of families than any "tangible" property they own, be it the house or car, and any property they can buy or sell, can mortgage and lend, bequeath or inherit. This raises the question of the rights of this new form of property and of the protection it needs.

A pension fund manager who converts to his own personal use monies meant to pay pensions to the plan's participants is clearly guilty of embezzlement. He would be laughed out of court if he were to argue that pension fund claims are, after all, not "property." Pension fund claims are surely "things of value" and are therefore treated as property in ordinary, everyday transactions. But when it comes to the greatest threat to pension fund claims, the analogy breaks down. Then we do not treat the pension fund claim as property. For unlike most other property, pension fund claims can be destroyed by forced compulsory misinvestment in non-productive rather than productive assets. This means, above all, that government can de facto expropriate pension fund claims, by forcing pension fund assets to be invested in what ostensibly are "safe investments" but are in reality compulsory levies and tributes unlikely ever to be repaid.

To "persuade" the pension funds of the employees of New York City in the fall of 1975 to sell the securities in prime companies they owned and to invest the proceeds in New York City bonds and notes was de facto "expropriation without compensation." The risk of default of these new City securities is surely so great that no trustee acting on his own could afford to take it. And the City's employees found out almost immediately that the "compensation" that was promised—that there would be no layoffs and no cuts in personnel, no cuts in City salaries and no cuts in pensions benefits—would not in fact be honored.

The all-but-compulsory conversion of the pension fund assets of New York City employees into subsidies to an insolvent City government was thus surely flagrant violation of the intent and spirit of the Fifth Amendment to the American Constitution. The Fifth Amendment expressly forbids the "taking of property without due process of law," and the taking of "private property for public use without just compensation." Yet the constitutional protection of property would clearly not be extended to the pension claim were the participants in New York City's pension funds to sue the City, the state government, or their own pension fund trustee. The pension fund claim is thus not yet legally recognized as "property."

It is also de facto "confiscation without compensation" if the employees of a business are being induced to invest pension fund assets exclusively or mainly in the stock of the company that employs them. For this not only means that the employees through their pension funds finance the company and its management rather than their own retirement. It means above all that at least half of the employees will eventually get no, or only a minimal, pension. Fewer than half of all businesses remain profitable or even survive over the period needed to build up a pension. According to the spirit of the Fifth Amendment, Senator Russell Long's bill passed in the fall of 1975 (mentioned earlier), which rewards with very significant tax subsidies such misinvestment of pension fund money, should therefore be declared unconstitutional at its first court test. It is governmental encouragement of confiscation "without due process." But it is unlikely that any court would yet consider the pension fund claim "property" within the meaning of the Fifth Amendment.

Outright expropriation of pension claims by government is most unlikely to come to pass. It would be about the most unpopular thing a government could do under pension fund socialism. But expropriation by compulsory misinvestment under government pressure or by government fiat is a real threat. Yet, under pension fund socialism the pension claim is fast becoming the basic economic right and the people's main asset. It is also the only way in which society can solve the central economic problem under the demographics of developed countries: the support of the older people who survive beyond working age. Pension fund claims are therefore not only "private property"; they are equally "social property."

This new form of property needs to be safeguarded against the threat to which it is uniquely vulnerable, the threat of compulsory misinvestment under government pressure, through government inducement, or by government fiat. The government which forces misinvestment of pension fund assets expropriates its own citizens and deprives them of what they have "commingled" their labor with. And it endangers the social and economic foundations of its own society.

But safeguarding this new property, the pension claim, against confiscation and expropriation by government is only the most immediate task. All told, we will have to think through the consequences for law, for economics, and for public policy, of the growing separation between "personal property," which is "standard of living," and property in the "means of production," which is rapidly becoming "social property" controlled by, and subject to, pension claims. In the United States "personal property" is largely exempt from taxation, except for real estate and inheritance taxes. But productive assets are heavily taxed through taxation of corporate income on dividend income, and on capital gains. Is this still the most equitable fiscal policy, when productive assets are increasingly the means to produce the support necessary for the retired, the older people? Do we need an additional, third classification for pension fund claims as "social property," beyond the two classes of "personal property" and "property in the means of production" which Marx defined 100 years ago? Is the pension fund claim basically different, i.e., an abstraction, of uncertain title and value, and a hypothetical share in collective "social" property rather than the specific "property" of a person? And what, then, are the rights and responsibilities of this peculiar new form of property?

But the first and immediate task which already confronts us is to extend the safeguards against governmental greed, governmental irresponsibility, and governmental thoughtlessness which the Fifth Amendment laid down for property generally to the new kind of "property": the pension claim and the assets underlying it which form the "social property" of the community.

Pension Fund Socialism and the Third World

Our discussion so far has been concerned with society and economy at home. But what are the implications of pension fund socialism for America's role, stance, and behavior in the outside world?

As far as the other developed countries are concerned, particularly the developed countries outside the Communist bloc, American pension fund socialism might provide the foundation for a new period of American leadership, *on condition, however, that we can solve the major problems which it poses.* The American response to the demographic changes and to the pressure for employee ownership of the means of production, that is pension fund socialism, is superior to any other solution developed by other Western countries or by Japan. It addresses foursquare the basic problem: the support of the older people. Yet it avoids the pitfalls of, for example, the Scandinavian approach, which would put the pension fund monies into one national fund and thus, in effect, freeze the economy and ensure that a substantial part of pension fund assets will be misinvested in the old, declining, obsolescent, or obsolete industries, to the detriment of economy and pension plan participants alike. And a system which, like the British or Japanese old age funds, bases future retirement pension primarily on government obligations is almost a prescription for permanent inflation.

Yet the potential which pension fund socialism offers for leadership in economic and social policy can become actual only when its major problems—those of capital formation, for instance, and of compulsory misinvestment of pension fund assets under government pressure—are solved. There is every reason for this country to make sure that its achievement is at least known and not ignored, as it has been so far. But we still have to demonstrate that we can handle the economic and social issues of pension fund socialism.

The America of pension fund socialism will find itself inevitably in conflict with the Third World countries. This will not be primarily a conflict of "system," and will only in part be based on the contrast between our wealth and their poverty, or on "white" versus "non-white." Primarily, it will be a question of a "generation gap." At the same time, pension fund socialism, and the demographics that underlie it, will create major opportunities for integration between America—and the other rich and developed countries—and the less developed countries of the Third World.

In the developed countries the older people, living beyond traditional working age, are emerging as the major center of demographic gravity. But most of the less developed countries have undergone during the same years a demographic revolution in the opposite direction. Birthrates in the poor undeveloped or developing countries have not been going up as seems to be widely believed. On the contrary, in every country on which we have information—and this means every country except Red China—birthrates have been in steady decline since the end of World War II; and in most of these countries quite a bit faster than they did in the West during comparable periods of economic growth and development. But infant mortality rates have been declining even faster. In the West, infant mortality rates—as I said earlier—did not decline sharply until the late nineteenth century, that is, until fairly late in the process of economic development. In the developing countries, the decline in infant mortality came before any substantial economic development.

Of every ten babies born in Mexico in 1940, only three

lived to adulthood. But of every ten babies born in Mexico in 1957 or 1958, seven or so are alive and adults today. Mexico's experience is typical. The percentages vary but the trend has been the same, especially in South America and throughout Asia.

The drop in infant mortality rates in the developing countries started right after World War II. But it did not gather momentum until the late fifties. The babies who did not die in the late fifties or early sixties are now reaching adulthood, and are becoming the center of demographic gravity throughout the developing countries. By 1985, the gap between birthrate and falling infant mortality rates should have narrowed sharply, and the center of demographic gravity in most developing countries will have started to move steadily upward. Where today, in most of these countries, half of the population is under sixteen, the mid-point should be around twenty in ten years time. But if these young adults have not found jobs in the meantime they will have become permanently a disenchanted, rebellious, alienated proletariat.

The developing countries thus face a decade during which jobs for very large numbers of young people entering the labor market will be the overriding challenge, and one for which neither of the "isms"—capitalism or communism—has an answer. The developing countries, above all, will face a decade in which the mood and temper of adolescents, their rhetoric, their values, and behavior, will characterize the mood, temper, rhetoric, values, and behavior of the entire society. On a much larger scale, the developing countries will come to resemble the "youth decade" of the developed countries during the late sixties and early seventies when the demographic center of gravity had shifted temporarily to the "babies" of the earlier baby boom. But this will happen (as we have seen) at just the time when the developed countries are shifting to new centers of demographic gravity: the young adults and, above all, older people.

The "youth rebellion" in the developing countries will have far more valid grievances than such rebellion in the developed countries ever had, despite Vietnam, racial discrimination, and the frustrations of a "bourgeois culture." But it will still be a "youth rebellion." Like any such rebellion, it will see the older people as the "enemy." And for "older people" today, read the societies of the developed countries, in which the older people are indeed the demographic center of gravity and likely to determine values, behavior, mood, and so on. The issues will ostensibly be "poverty," "exploitation," "colonialism," "racism," and "imperialism." The central fact, however, will be the "generation gap"—with all the friction, raucousness, violence, and frustration this engenders on both sides.

Such misunderstanding, mutual antagonism, and frustration on both sides will be further aggravated by the growing dependence of most of the developing countries on the one absolutely essential supply which only North America and particularly the United States can provide: food. The petroleum cartel, whatever its effects on the developed countries, has had a devastating impact on the ability of the developing countries to increase food production. It raised fertilizer prices three- to fivefold, just at the very time when increased fertilizer use was becoming most crucial to the developing world and when it had acquired the ability to raise food output, provided only that fertilizer —which means, in essence, crude oil—would be available in large quantities and at low price. At the same time, North America alone of all the major regions in the world has the capacity, the capital, and the skills to increase supplies of food substantially, on the basis of existing or known technology, crops, crop yields, and tools. That America will thus wield increasing control and power can only heighten the feelings of frustration and impotence among the "youth rebels" of the Third World.

Yet the "generation gap" between the developed countries—especially the United States—and the developing countries also paradoxically offers a unique opportunity for economic integration. Developed countries and developing ones are becoming complementary in their job opportunities and their job needs. This almost makes mandatory an economic integration under which the job needs of the developing world are matched with the labor deficiencies of the developed world, to the benefit of both. Indeed, the development is already fully under way, though still only in its earliest stages.

The developed countries face an absolute drop in the number of young people entering the labor force, and fewer and fewer of the newcomers will be available for manual, particularly manufacturing, work. This can no longer be remedied by large-scale immigration of people from pre-industrial, rural areas into the industrialized cities, whether from the farm in Japan, the Deep South in the United States, or from the countries of the Mediterranean into Western and Northern Europe. Neither in Japan nor in the United States is there still a reservoir of under-employed and skimpily schooled young people on the land. And the countries of Northern and Western Europe have reached the cultural and economic limits of their capacity to absorb immigrants from different cultures. All of them are restricting further immigration and are indeed trying to send back some of their "guest workers." The developed countries will therefore increasingly have to concentrate on those areas in which capital, management, advanced technology, and a good, perhaps even abundant, supply of knowledge workers results in higher productivity and greater output.

By contrast, many of the developing countries will have a surplus of exactly the kind of workers who are going to be in shortest supply in the developed countries: young people available for unskilled or semi-skilled manufacturing jobs. The young people who now enter the labor force are not highly schooled or highly skilled in most of these countries. But they are available in the urban centers; South America, as well as most of Asia, is urbanized today, with three quarters or so of their people living in cities. These people have proven themselves ready for the culture of the modern factory. In this respect they are way ahead of the workers whom the developed countries imported in such large numbers from the pre-industrial, rural areas— whether sharecroppers from the South, farm boys and girls from Japan's North, or unemployed farm laborers from Portugal, Turkey, or Morocco.

Capital, technology, and even management, the developing countries could in theory import; but one prerequisite of employment and economic development that most of them cannot supply themselves or obtain through aid or borrowing is the access to markets. Only the developed countries can offer the markets and the distributive systems without which none but the largest of the developing countries—Brazil, for instance—could develop fast. For development requires a big enough market to make possible manufacturing industry of adequate scale. Few, if any, of the developing countries could gain access to the markets of the developed countries by themselves. This is not a matter of "exporting." It requires a marketing organization, knowledge of the local markets, their customers and distributive channels, of marketing finance and marketing management. It can only be done on the spot, essentially by people who are part of the local market, know it, are experienced and successful in it—that is, by marketing and distributive businesses, headquartered and managed in the developed countries. It is no accident that none of the Arab petroleum producers shows any desire to replace the marketing systems of the large international oil companies. With all their money, they could not do it.

What the Germans used to call *"Veredelungsverkehr"* (no other language has a word for it, though the literal English translation is "upgrading trade") may thus become the dominant mode of international economics. The developed countries will concentrate on those stages of production in which they have the advantage. These are the stages that require capital; for the more of a capital shortage there is, the more will capital be concentrated in the developed countries. These are, further, the stages that require technology, management, and knowledge workers on the one hand, and marketing knowledge, marketing and distributive systems, and marketing finance in the developed countries on the other hand. The developing countries will increasingly take on those jobs which are primarily labor-intensive. That their wages are lower is not the major factor. Indeed, the productivity of labor in low-wage countries tends, as a rule, to be low and labor costs per unit of output to be rather high. "Low wages," in other words, are usually an illusion and do not mean low labor costs. What matters is that the developing countries have the available manpower.

One example of such *Veredelungsverkehr* is illustrated by electronic instruments such as hand-held calculators, essentially assemblies of semi-conductors. Semi-conductors are only produced in developed countries, particularly in the United States or by American companies. They require very high technology, constant innovation, very high capital investment, and management of great competence. But the assembly of the semi-conductors into finished electronic products is largely carried out in countries that have an abundance of manual labor, such as Hong Kong, Singapore, or Indonesia. The selling is then done in the developed countries by the businesses that make the semi-conductors and design the products, to distributors they know and to whom they have direct access.

This sounds like "big company stuff." In fact, many successful participants in this *Veredelungsverkehr,* in the electronic industry, for one, are small businesses. In some ways a small business has an advantage. It is more flexible—and *Veredelungsverkehr* requires high flexibility. But, of course, the large manufacturing company in the developed country also is increasingly forced into international integration, which meshes the resources and advantages of the developed countries with the resources and needs of the developing world. Tomorrow's "multinational" will increasingly not be a company with factories everywhere, owned and controlled by a central head office located in New York, London, Tokyo, or Düsseldorf. Rather, it will be the manager of a worldwide system of autonomous, if not independent, businesses which are integrated in production and distribution. Its role will be to supply capital, technology, management, and access to the markets. The very feature of the "multinational" which today is under most severe attack in the developing countries, namely, that it integrates production and makes allocation decisions, may be what the developing countries need the most. Indeed, it may be the one essential requirement for them to survive the next ten years without risking widespread famine and social collapse.

It is thus not only in the domestic areas of the developed country, and especially of the United States, that the demands of pension fund socialism will collide head-on with the beliefs, slogans, and passions of the recent past. The developing countries will be faced with excruciating choices between popular rhetoric and social reality. It will be a major emotional problem for many of them that the developed countries are going to be so clearly in the driver's seat, if only because of the food surpluses they alone will control. And it will be a major political problem for them to adjust their nationalist commitments and convictions to the demands of economic integration. Yet the countries that can make this adjustment—the tiny Chinese communities of Hong Kong and Taiwan and Singapore have so far done it the most successfully—are likely to provide the most jobs, the highest income for the most people, and the biggest opportunities for economic growth and social development.

For the United States, and for every other developed country, economic integration, while of obvious and clear benefit, also presents major problems. It can be taken for granted that the labor unions will oppose it. They will have a legitimate point. The businesses and industries which no longer can be kept alive by the population base of the developed countries may not deserve much sympathy, but the workers in these industries do. They are likely to be the older workers, largely the ones with limited skills and little education. The new jobs will be knowledge jobs. Unemployment caused by the shift may be quite low overall, but it may be concentrated among older workers in a small number of communities with few alternative employment opportunities. The older labor-intensive industries cannot be maintained in the developed countries; there would not be enough manual labor available to keep them going, whatever the subsidy. The shift to economic integration with the labor-surplus countries of the developing world therefore needs to be encouraged rather than opposed. But there is need also for a policy which retrains, relocates, and supports the displaced—especially the older displaced workers in those industries which developed countries can no longer adequately staff.

Relations between the developed countries and the developing countries thus will make tremendous demands on both. The demographic changes demand policies which fly in the face of traditional economic nationalism, of traditional international economics, and of the traditional concepts of "economic development." Yet the shift is already under way and rapidly gathering momentum. However painful such economic integration will be, it offers the best, if not the only chance for assuaging the "generation conflict" between the "cynical adults" of the developed countries and the "brash youngsters" of the developing ones.

The most important point about the new demands on our social institutions and the new social issues is not their novelty. Nor is it their difficulty, though some of them will indeed be hard to satisfy. Above all, it is that they are diametrically opposed to the mood, the slogans, the rhetoric, which still dominate the headlines and shape policies today. But this only means that the "opinion makers"—journalists, politicians and academics—have not yet perceived pension fund socialism or the demographic changes that underlie it. Our ability and willingness to alter our perception and to accept these changes as fundamental, as real, and as accomplished facts will largely determine whether we can master the new social demands and whether America can shape an effective social policy during the next decade.

4. The Political Lessons and Political Issues of Pension Fund Socialism

What Became of the "Isms"?

No one, twenty-five years ago, anticipated that the pension funds would come to own American business. But if anybody, whatever his political or economic persuasion, had foreseen this outcome, he would surely have predicted that it would have profound impact on the "system." Power relationships would change radically. The role and function of management, if not our institutions themselves, would be altered drastically. The basic politics of the country would somehow shift from top to bottom.

None of these things has happened so far. In fact, the coming of "socialism" to America has had very little impact on American institutions, American power structure, American politics, even on American political rhetoric. Yet we have succeeded in shaping a genuine "socialism" linked to, and indeed made possible by, a genuine "capitalism"— if by "capitalism" is meant resource allocation in and through a market mechanism.

Pension fund socialism has its opportunities and its problems. It raises new policy issues. The demographic changes, and especially the survival of large numbers of people beyond working age, have far-reaching consequences. But none of these issues is primarily that of "socialism." As far as its impact on the "system" is concerned, pension fund socialism can only be called trivial.

Socialism trivial? The very idea seems preposterous, considering the fervor with which Socialist panaceas of all kinds are being embraced by all critics of the "system." But maybe this is the fervor of despair, the fervor of *"Credo quia absurdum"* in which the "true believer" always takes refuge when his millennial dream comes up against reality. For that reality—and the great lesson of the American experiment—is that the alternatives today are not those of the nineteenth century,* of "capitalism" and "socialism" or even of "individualism" and "collectivism."

The crucial moment in the disintegration of "socialism" as the alternative to the "system" was probably August 1, 1914, when the proletariat, despite its highly organized and disciplined Socialist parties—the dominant parties in France, Germany, Austria, and Italy—enthusiastically joined an "imperialist war" rather than make common cause with its working-class brethren across national boundaries.

But the decisive event, the event that destroys the intellectual foundations of "socialism" as a creed, is surely American pension fund socialism. For if the American experience proves anything it is that the fundamental conflict in the developed countries—for all that it invokes the old battle cries and waves the old banners—is not about "capi-

*A conclusion that Daniel Bell reached from entirely different premises in *The End of Ideology* (New York: Basic Books, 1960). See also my book *The Landmarks of Tomorrow* (New York: Harper & Row, 1950), and *The Age of Discontinuity* (New York: Harper & Row, 1969).

talism" and "socialism" at all; it is about power. It is a conflict between a decentralization of power, in which a substantial number of pluralist power centers make decisions, thus leaving a meaningful sphere of freedom for the individual; and a monopoly of power by a small clique one might call the "military-intellectual complex," which likes to usurp for its own use the term "socialism," and which keeps itself in power by buying, through "transfer payments," the support of the less productive or non-productive groups. Marx would have called it a cabal of the "lumpen intellectuals" and the "lumpen proletariat." Even that might be secondary compared to the "generation gap" —rooted, in large measure, in demographics rather than in the "system"—between a developed and largely white world in which the increase in older surviving people is the main demographic phenomenon, and a less developed or underdeveloped world, largely non-white, where the basic phenomenon is the drop in infant mortality and the resulting explosive growth of young people (little trained and little skilled) to be fed and provided with jobs.

The "isms" will of course continue to be invoked; nothing dies more slowly than an old slogan. But policies can no longer be based on them. They appeal to passion while no longer providing modes of rational action, let alone conceptual frames for political thought. Whoever, from now on in the American political context, speaks of "socialism" either means nothing at all or he means pension fund socialism, in which "socialism" co-exists with "capitalism" and is, in fact, mutually dependent on it. He means a system in which the "means of production" have become "social property" and thereby support personal property rights and personal incomes. He speaks of a system in which the workers own the "means of production" and therefore have to demand a high rate of profitability. This is—to reiterate—rigorous, orthodox, "textbook socialism." The socialism of Marxist theory has indeed been realized, and for the first time, on American soil. But in realizing genuine pension fund socialism, the American development has invalidated and made meaningless the nineteenth century's "isms."

The Effectiveness of Non-governmental Policies

If the "isms" are the legacy of the nineteenth century, the unquestioning belief that government, and government alone, is the effective organ of social policy and social action is the legacy of the early years of this century. This is the specific twentieth-century "ism." And this, too, is disproven by the American development. For pension fund socialism emerged without benefit of government programs or government policy. It was the result of pluralist, voluntary, community action, largely on the part of non-governmental, private-sector institutions.

Not many people today, in this or any other developed country, still believe fervently in governmental "programs." Indeed, the pervasive cynicism regarding the capacity of government to deliver on its programs—other than to build a big bureaucracy and spend a good deal of money—is a real danger. But while our generation has lost the almost unlimited faith in government which prevailed in the thirties and then again in the sixties, nothing else has taken its place. There seems to be no alternative.

The fact that non-governmental action has produced a profound change by means of the pension funds therefore teaches an important lesson. None of the governmental programs for economic or social change put into effect in any developed country within the last thirty years—since

World War II and the Japanese Land Reform which followed it—has had anywhere near the effectiveness that the pension fund movement has had. In fact, one might without much exaggeration say that it is the *only* economic and social program of the last thirty years that has truly produced results and delivered what it promised. The pension fund movement is not "individualism" *à la* Herbert Hoover. Pension funds are collectives. And the agents are other collectives, the large employing organizations. But they are "non-governmental" and, in that sense, "private." They offer one example of the efficacy of using the existing private non-governmental institutions of our "society of organizations" for the formulation and achievement of social goals and the satisfaction of social needs.

The American pension fund development also demonstrates why such non-governmental, pluralist, private-sector action is likely to be more effective in developing social policy and social programs than governmental action. The pension funds were first developed in response to needs which had not yet become "issues." In fact, when the pension funds began twenty-five years ago, nobody quite saw the imminent demographic shift and with it the need for developing a mechanism to support an older, retired population. The solution, in other words, was found before there was a "problem." As a result, the solution could be developed to fit the specific problem rather than abstract doctrine or theory.

The pluralist approach also made possible experimentation, out of which the most appropriate one emerged—the GM approach, in which pensions are handled through an "investment" mechanism. This then made possible a major social transformation without "revolution," indeed without much ado. It made it possible to test a number of different approaches and to curtail, if not abandon, the ones which turned out not to work no matter how attractive they looked as a plan. Thirty years ago, before GM developed its approach, industry-wide and union-managed pension plans clearly looked like the solution. Considering how poorly these plans have performed, it is obvious now that they were not "the solution." If there had not been the experimentation and testing of pluralism which used the non-governmental private institutions of society to develop and test alternative approaches, we might by now be committed to the wrong plan and the wrong solution. And the rapid deterioration of Social Security into a deficit-ridden welfare agency also shows that the purely governmental approach to old age security would not, at least in this country, produce either the right results or the permanent "solution."

These are important lessons, doubly so at this time when the infallibility of government and governmental programs is no longer accepted or even credible.

The first area to which the lesson of the pension fund achievement must be applied is probably that of the pension funds themselves. Social Security, as has been said before, is in serious trouble, drifting toward insolvency—in part because of inflation; in part because it has been subverted into a "welfare" program; and in part because of the inflexibility and rigidity of its retirement provisions, which force people into involuntary retirement who still want to work and to earn. It will be only too tempting for the politicians to try to "solve" the Social Security problem by destroying the pension funds' achievement, expropriating pension fund assets to restore Social Security's financial health. This would not solve the Social Security crisis. But it might destroy, or at least seriously damage, the pension funds and with them the retirement security of the American worker.

Surely, if the pension fund achievement teaches us anything, it is that the Social Security crisis would best be handled by moving as much as possible of Social Security into the private sector, to the existing non-governmental pension funds. This would still leave Social Security with the "problems" which a private pension system, a system based on annuities and investments, cannot solve: the problems of the "old age proletariat" and of the small group of people outside the Social Security system; in other words, the straight welfare problems. But these are manageable by themselves, though money can only assuage them. What we have to guard against is the opposite approach, which sacrifices a functioning pension fund system to the marginal "problem areas." Yet this is what will surely be advocated and attempted.

The same lesson also applies to health care. Uniform, central-government, all-inclusive "national health care" has lost a great deal of its luster since it has become apparent that the British National Health Service is in disarray—largely as a result of political mismanagement which, for thirty years, has deprived the British Health Service of the capital funds it needs. Perhaps we will get over the reverse snobbery, so popular today, which brags, quite falsely, that health care in America costs the most and produces the least. People may come to realize that health care takes about the same proportion of national income in all developed countries, and produces no more in any of them than it does in the United States. Perhaps it may even be no longer grossly unpopular to point out that no one else knows how to tackle the two areas in which American health care is clearly deficient: the delivery of health care to the very poor and the delivery of health care in sparsely settled rural regions.

Yet there is still a danger that, in approaching health

care, we forget the lesson of the pension funds and try to abolish, rather than use, the existing pluralist (though admittedly not very orderly) health care institutions that we have, both for delivering health care and for paying for it. If the pension fund achievement teaches us anything, it is that health care, like pension funds, can only be treated with any hope for performance and success if the autonomous pluralist institutions of society are encouraged to carry the main burden and to develop competing, alternative approaches. Only the marginal areas that are not "insurable" should be assigned to governmental effort.

The same lesson must be applied to education. We need to maintain the pluralism of tax-supported and private education in colleges and universities, which has been one of the strengths of the American system of higher education. Yet there is real danger that the private, non-governmental college and university will go under as it is forced to compete, without much tax money, against heavily subsidized governmental institutions at a time when enrollments are no longer rising. The remedy is simple: a revival of the concept that worked so well right after World War II in the GI Bill of Rights, when the institution which the returning veteran selected was paid a modest but reasonable stipend, whether it was a private or a public body.

The approach might well be extended to secondary and even elementary education. The rationale for a single educational approach and program imposed on all the schools in a given school district disappeared when the country became suburban. If there are five or six elementary schools within the same suburban community—and there are that many in most suburbs today—there is no reason to have only one approach to education. There could be two or three to fit the different requirements of different children, or the preferences of their parents. And we know today that it is not true that there is one "right" educational system or philosophy for every youngster. This rationalized the necessities of yesterday, when most people lived in a small village that could afford only one school and often only one teacher. Then, indeed, there had to be one educational approach and uniformity. There also had to be a monopoly, otherwise the school could not have been supported. But there is no reason today why we should not have choice and competition—and indeed every reason for both. Otherwise we are most unlikely to develop the educational approaches, the curricula, the pedagogy, and the schools that we need so badly to enable youngsters again to learn and teachers again to teach.

Individual areas of application are less important than the lesson itself, however. It is fashionable these days to speak of the "mixed economy" in which a large "public sector" co-exists with, and lives off, a "private sector." But we also have, or should have, a "mixed society," in which we can use both the specific virtues and capacities of government and the specific strengths of non-governmental autonomous social institutions. Government is needed to make policy. It is needed to *do* a few things which only government can do—defense, for instance, or the dispensation of justice. But government is primarily not a "doer." It is, rather, a policy maker, a vision maker, a goal setter. Policy is always dogmatic and requires convictions, logical reasons, rigid positions, large generalizations. But "doing" requires willingness and ability to experiment; "programs" must be pragmatic, else they fail. Government, however, is ill suited to the demands of pragmatism. So far as the responses to either need or opportunity are concerned, we must be able to mobilize the resources of the non-governmental institutions of society. This is not "individualism"; it is non-governmental "collectivism." At least the pension-fund achievement demonstrates an alternative to the dependence on government which has characterized most of the last half century, and which, to many people, despite their admitted doubt, disenchantment, and cynicism, still appears the only policy. If, indeed, we can develop the "mixed society" in which autonomous non-governmental institutions carry out the doing work of needed programs, we may come to look upon the emergence of the pension fund in America as a turning point in political theory and political practice.

The Myth of Affluence

The final political lesson of pension fund socialism is that affluence is a myth. It is almost twenty years since John Kenneth Galbraith made "affluence" (until then a rather esoteric term) into a household word. In his book, *The Affluent Society* (published in 1958), Galbraith had two major theses. One was that the American economy had reached the point where there were essentially no limits to what it could produce. Economic restraints had disappeared or were becoming irrelevant. Therefore, Galbraith maintained, the traditional parsimony in respect to governmental and public services was not only unwarranted but shocking. He contrasted the "affluence" of the "private sector," or the way most Americans live, with the "squalor" of the public sector—at a time when, according to him, there were no economic limits to what the public sector could or should spend.

No other economic text found such immediate response. Galbraith's basic concepts became effective and the cornerstone for American economic policies within two years. The two axioms on which American public policy has been based since the election of John F. Kennedy to the presidency are, although simplified, the axioms of Galbraith's book: Economically, America can afford anything; and public-sector spending can, and should, be increased as fast as possible.

There is no parallel in government history—certainly not in peacetime—to the expansion of public spending in the United States in the last fifteen years. When Galbraith published his book, the federal government's budget was $70 billions. By 1976, the only question was whether the official budget ceiling of $395 billions was too low, and whether any ceiling could be set and observed at all. States and cities have increased their expenditures perhaps even faster. Fully adjusted for the declining purchasing power of the dollar, which was of course largely caused by this explosion of governmental spending and governmental deficits, we have increased governmental expenditures three- to fourfold within fifteen years, or doubled governmental spending, on average, every five or six years. And this even though defense spending—the main expenditure item of 1958—has been going down steadily as a proportion of the budget, as a proportion of national income, and, for ten years now, in real non-inflated dollars as well. The results are perhaps not exactly what Galbraith predicted. Maybe the term "squalor" which he applied to the government institutions and services of 1958 applies more appropriately to some governmental institutions and services of 1975—New York City, for instance; the U.S. Post Office; or the federal housing program. But if so, it surely is not for want of money.

Galbraith's second premise, that the American economy had become so "affluent" as to be able to afford any socially desirable expenditure, was even more widely accepted. Since the appearance of *The Affluent Society*, the question: "Can we afford it?" has increasingly come to be considered irrelevant, if not stupid. The question instead is: "Do we want it?" And if the answer is: "Yes," it has been taken for granted that we can afford it.

But nothing is quite as painfully obvious today as that we cannot afford a great many things that may be desirable. And nothing is quite so obvious today as that "affluence" is a delusion. The limits, the restraints, the deficiencies of America's capacity to produce are rapidly becoming the central problems of economic and social policy. Both the administration and the Congress accept that budget making has to start with a ceiling on expenditures based on what the country can afford. The financial crises of the big cities, beginning with New York, or the threatened crisis of Social Security, have their roots in our inability to afford all we would like to have.

What matters is not that Galbraith's confident assumption of "affluence" has been proven wrong, but why. Galbraith and the economists and politicians following him failed to take into account the demographic change. Underlying many of the major "crises" of public policy today is the emergence of the very large number of older people who have to be supported out of the production of those at work. The root cause of New York City's problems, and of those of the other large cities and states, is the unfunded pension claims and especially unfunded past-service liabilities for pension claims. This is also the root cause of the looming capital shortage. And it is the main reason why the taxpayer, who now sees one-fifth of his earnings taken away from him to support Social Security and pension payments, resists further taxes. Whether the demographic change should have been foreseen in 1958 or 1960 is debatable; it certainly could have been seen in the mid-sixties, when governmental expenditures began to expand at an explosive rate.

Now in the mid-seventies it is clear to all but the most

willfully blind that the central economic fact of the American economy is not "affluence"; it is the need for productivity to support the older people beyond working age. In the next ten years this will, inexorably, become an even greater need as the dependency ratio becomes less and less favorable. "Austerity," the newly fashionable term favored by such "populist liberals" as Governor Brown in California, Governor Dukakis in Massachusetts, or Governor Straub in Oregon, is as much hyperbole and rhetorical exaggeration as "affluence" was yesterday. What passes for "austerity" in the United States would still be extravagance in the richest of the other developed countries, and beyond the wildest dreams of imagination in fairly well-off "developing" countries. But the very fact that the term has gained such wide currency and has such strong voter appeal clearly reveals that the limits of economic resources and economic production, rather than their abundance, is becoming the central issue in American economic policy.

Of all the lessons of pension fund socialism and the demographic change underlying it, this will be the hardest one to accept. Everybody is in favor of "austerity"—as long as it means that somebody else's pet program is being cut back, or at least not expanded any further. But the true meaning of the lesson is that *all* our priorities are in need of change, from what is desirable to what is necessary. Above all, we must accept that the support of the older population is the first priority of public policy, even though it can be obtained only through performance in the private sector. For all our talk about "austerity," neither the politicians nor the public are yet ready to accept its implications.

But fundamentally we have no choice. There is no escape from the conclusion that "affluence" is a myth, and that the reality of the American economy is extreme pressure on productive capacity to produce the goods and services needed to support a fast-growing older population. The only choice is whether this need will be recognized or not. It will not go away by being ignored.

This leads us to the political issues which the emergence of pension fund socialism and the demographic change underlying it will create, or at least move into the center of American politics.

Welfare Society versus Welfare State

In the fiscal year ending June 30, 1975, welfare spending by all governmental agencies in the United States—federal, state, and local—amounted, according to the Social Security administration, to $287 billion. Non-governmental spending on social welfare amounted, according to the same source, to another $100 billion, for a total welfare bill of some $390 billion.

This was by no means the total expenditure on public services. Government spent another $200 to 250 billion, including $100 billion for defense, with the rest spread over a multitude of services, such as the Post Office deficit, the building of highways, subsidies to transportation, the National Parks, or water supply and sewers in the cities. In addition, the public directly pays around $100 billion for services which, in most other developed countries, are part of the government budget: two-thirds of health care and that part of education that is not tax-supported, such as parochial schools or private colleges. The total expenditure for "public" services, which are in effect "transfer payments" from the wage earner to the public sector, thus came to $700 billion, or close to 50 percent of the gross national product of $1,450 billion.

This, by the way, is as high a proportion as the public

expenditure of any other country, and higher than that of most other developed countries. It makes a lie of the often-heard assertion that the American pays less to the public sector than do the citizens of other countries. Only in Sweden, it would seem, does as large a share of the GNP go into public services as it does in the United States. Every place else the public-service share of the GNP is lower, whether the government be a labor government as currently in Britain, or a conservative government as in Japan—and in most countries it is a good deal lower.

The $400 billion of welfare expenditures run to almost one-third of the GNP. All these "welfare payments" go to one "minority" or another: the blacks, the poor, the Mexican-Americans, and so on. The older retired people are a larger "minority" than any of these, yet their support through Social Security pensions and payments from employers' pension plans takes the smallest share of the welfare expenditures—some $100 billion. And the old are the only minority which provides for its own support during its working years, through its contributions to Social Security and to pension plans. This may not make it more "deserving"; what are the criteria anyhow? But if the old socialist slogan: "From each according to his ability and to each according to his needs" can be taken as the most liberal definition of who is "deserving," then the older employees who, after a lifetime of work, reach retirement age, should rank high. In addition, in sharp contrast to every other minority group, the older population has a very large constituency outside its own ranks. Every employee over fifty, and surely everyone over fifty-five, is a potential member who expects to join the ranks of the old retired people in the not-very-distant future.

The $100 billion or so which today go to the support of the older, retired population and their survivors are well below what we already need to spend each year. As has been said before, a great many retirement plans—beginning with Social Security, and including most of the retirement plans of local governments, but also some corporate plans—are grossly underfunded, especially in respect to past-service liability. If we fully funded the retirement obligations we incur, we would need something closer to $140–150 billion a year, that is, half as much again as we now budget for. And over the next ten years, the number of people who will have to be supported because they have reached retirement age, or are the late-middle-aged survivors of deceased employees, will increase by one-third. Between now and 1985 the total needed to support the older, retired people and their survivors, and to pay back the accumulated deficit for past-service liability, will come to an annual burden of at least $175 billion if not $200 billion, without any adjustment for inflation.

There is no provision for this expansion, least of all in Social Security. Yet all the other welfare budgets are designed for rapid expansion. Government programs, in particular, are "locked in" and not "controllable," or so the political wisdom of today affirms.

The United States is thus set on a collision course between the promises it has made to its older citizens and its commitments to special-interest groups, other minorities which individually are much less numerous and politically hardly more powerful, though more visible and more vocal. It is not very likely that the promises to both groups can be honored. To do so would mean a social welfare expenditure 50 to 60 percent higher than that of 1975. Even if the economy grows very fast, the welfare expenditures would grow much faster; by the early eighties, if we continue on the present course, welfare expenditures alone without a penny spent on all other needs (whether defense, health care, education, transportation, or the environment) would take half even of a substantially larger GNP.

The older population is not part of the "welfare state"; it is self-supporting. Today's employees provide for their own future support by supporting today's retired people. They are a "welfare society." The rest of the welfare expenditure is the "welfare state," that is, transfer of income from producers to non-producers without any return to the producers. Are the two compatible? Can we afford both together? And which, in the event of a collision, should be given priority? This will increasingly become a central political issue.

The initial response on the part of the politician when confronted with such a situation is always to ask for more taxes. This was predictably the politicians' response to the New York City crisis, which was the first major skirmish in the coming battle between welfare society and welfare state —in this case between the support of the retirement plans for New York City's employees and the expenditures on a large number of other "minorities." But higher taxes has already proven to be a totally inadequate response. In the first place, higher taxes are likely to aggravate rather than alleviate the disease—as they undoubtedly will in New York City. They can only hasten the departure of producers, whether individuals or businesses. Secondly, they are no longer a tolerable remedy. The taxpayer in this country, and indeed in all developed countries, is going on strike. He already carries a heavy burden for the support of the older people, which he himself hopes and expects to join someday. He will not, and perhaps cannot, pay more to support the "welfare state" of the other "minorities" which he has no intention of joining at any time.

The alternative political response to the clash of welfare society and welfare state is to allow inflation. But this is a short-lived expedient. Every group immediately attempts to "catch up," which only fuels inflation without resolving the problem.

Higher taxes and inflation may postpone the confrontation until "after the next election"—but surely not much beyond. They only make the problem harder to resolve and the confrontation more bitter, more divisive, more intractable. We are close to the point—if we have not reached it already—where the producing employed people refuse to accept still higher taxes while the older people, beginning with the older people at work, refuse to accept more inflation. Then there will be no escape from the disagreeable fact that either the welfare society of the older people or the welfare state of the "deserving minorities" will have to be cut back, and fairly sharply at that.

For twenty years American demographics has moved in one direction: toward the emergence of a near-majority of people who are themselves of retirement age, or close enough to have a major stake in their pensions. During the same period, American social policy has moved by contrast toward a "politics of conscience" that advocates the support of the "disadvantaged," the "underprivileged," the "deserving." Eventually, such a split becomes unbearable —two such contradictory commitments exceed what can be borne. How soon this point will be reached is anybody's guess, but the figures indicate that it cannot be more than a few years off.

If this clash were to be decided by voting power alone, it would almost certainly be won by the older people. With their support among the middle-aged at work, they could marshal by themselves a near-majority of the voting population. To be sure, they still lack a standard bearer. Politicians, however, are adept at switching their allegiance to the side that has the bigger battalions.

The older people may also have a good strong case in conscience. Not only have they paid for their future retirement, so that they are not asking for handouts but for fulfillment of the terms of a contract which they have satisfied fully and in good faith. They could also claim that for many years society, and especially governmental employers, have defaulted on their contractual obligations—through non-funding and underfunding, for instance—and that they only claim something they were promised all along and should have received all along. The law has long recognized a special "workingman's lien" which a worker obtains by giving service, and which ranks ahead of all other creditors. What the older, retired population has is, in effect, a "workingman's lien" on the social product; they have done the work. And it would be a rash metaphysician who would be willing to decide whether a "workingman's lien" deserves priority over the claims of "charity."

This is, of course, sheer speculation. What is not speculation but near-certainty is that there will be a collision between the claims of the "welfare society," created by the demographic changes and operating through pension fund socialism, and the demands of the "welfare state."

Equality versus Equality

The pension funds emerged at the same time, though quite independently, as the drive for equality of opportunity generally and equality of opportunity and rights for the country's "minorities" specifically. As a result, discrimination in employment on account of age is now prohibited by law, along with discrimination by race, religion, or sex. But the most stringent discriminations in employment on account of age are the penalties of the Social Security laws on working beyond age sixty-five, and the compulsory retirement at an arbitrary age incorporated into most pension plans. This may well be the most flagrant "denial of equal opportunity" in the United States today; it is certainly the most widely practiced one.

In the sixties the drive for equality shifted focus from the racial minorities to women. Before the decade of the seventies comes to an end, the Constitutional Amendment guaranteeing complete equality to women may well be ratified. So far Social Security has not been touched; yet it is the most "sexist" of our major institutions. It glaringly discriminates against the married working woman, who has to choose between receiving the retirement benefits she has paid for out of her earnings, and receiving the retirement benefits for spouses of retired workers or their widows which her husband has paid for out of his income. The household in which two people work is taxed twice for retirement, without any concession for a married couple filing jointly which the ordinary income tax or capital gains tax provides. One of the two retirement incomes the couple has paid for is forfeited and expropriated by the Social Security system—usually that of the married working woman.

Nor is this historical accident. To be sure, when Social Security was first designed in the twenties, the labor-force participation of married women was a fraction of what it is today; the priority was to provide for the non-working widow or the spouse of the retired worker. But when Social Security was enacted, in the mid-thirties, the discrimination against the married working woman was deliberate and was carried far beyond what had been originally intended. Then, in the middle of the Great Depression, the "two-earner family" was considered undesirable; and the woman who worked though married to a man with a job was condemned as "antisocial," taking away jobs from men and income from other families, their wives, and children. American Social Security legislation thus reflects a deliberate bias against the working woman. Yet women are a decided majority among the older population, and women who have worked are in turn almost a majority among older women.

The rapid expansion of the number of older people and of the pension funds also coincides with the emergence of a strong militant drive for equality of income and condition —as opposed to equality of rights and opportunity—for everyone but especially for "disadvantaged minorities." Egalitarianism has become a driving passion in developed countries. Only nationalism has even stronger impact on the political mood of modern societies. But of all "minorities," that of the older, retired people is the one most universally unequal in its income. The employed worker at age sixty-four years and 360 days is "privileged" compared to the "minorities" with which the popular rhetoric of egalitarianism usually deals, the poor or the poor blacks, for instance. Ten days later, having been retired at age sixty-five, his income is half or less what it had been only a week earlier.

The first suit challenging the discrimination against married working women in the Social Security laws was filed in late 1975. The first bill to outlaw mandatory retirement for age alone was introduced into the Congress in early 1976. From now on equality for older people—and especially for older women—should become an increasingly potent and popular demand as the number of older people increases sharply over the next decade. It may come to rival in the late seventies and early eighties "Women's Lib" as a political and legal issue. For older, retired people (and people of retirement age who don't want to retire) are by far the largest "minority"—larger than the poor, the blacks, or any of the other minority groups in American (or in any other developed) society. They are also the only rapidly growing "disadvantaged" group. This minority cuts across all other lines; it is the most representative. It is the one minority which everyone hopes he will join. Getting old may not be highly desirable, but most people prefer it to the alternative. The members of this minority are disadvantaged through no fault of their own; yet they also are not "disadvantaged" through somebody else's "fault." No one else is benefitting at their expense, taking anything away from them, oppressing them, or exploiting them. They are not, as all other disadvantaged minorities (or majorities) are held to be, the "victims of society." On the contrary, they are the "successes of society." Yet they are a genuine minority and suffer from real income inequality.

In a society as sensitive to inequality as ours professes itself to be, the inequality of the older, retired people simply will not go unnoticed. These people have the numbers and the voting power to make themselves heard; the egalitarian temper of the times ensures that they will be listened to.

Furthermore, the inequality of this group is fundamentally different from that of any other. And the traditional prescriptions for dealing with inequality are either inappropriate here or can only aggravate it.

The standard prescription for inequality throughout history was to create "equality of opportunity," in other words, to provide everybody with equal access to rights, to jobs, to education, and so on. Equality of opportunity would, of course, not lead to equality of reward. Unequal performance and unequal abilities would be rewarded unequally. This is what moral philosophers have always meant by "justice." But in the first place, removing the barriers to equality of opportunity would result in greatly increased social and economic performance (the argument goes back to Adam Smith and, well before him, to David Hume, if not to the Old Testament). It would thus provide the means for "compassion," for dealing with those people and groups who are so seriously lacking in ability as to need social support. And it would, of course, if fully realized, make the problem of inequality a manageable one—confining it to those whose "inequality of condition" results from true, inborn, irreversible, and serious inequality of endowment.

The most consistent exponent of this traditional approach was probably Karl Marx. "Socialism" to Marx was the means—the only means—to bring about true "equality of opportunity" for everyone. This would then release such an outburst of productivity and production as to usher in the age of true abundance. Then, and only then, could the problem of "inequality of condition" resulting from a lack of "native ability" be dealt with; and then it would present no problem. Anyone, however, who demanded "equality of condition" (e.g., of income) before that time was a "counter-revolutionary" and an enemy of true equality—the issue over which Marx broke with all the egalitarians of his time, as in his celebrated and savage battle with Bakunin and the Anarchists.

But all along there has been another approach which focuses on "equality of condition," and especially on "equality of income," as the true equality, and considers "equality of opportunity" to be itself extreme inequality. In the classical expression of this approach, superior ability, being after all an accident of birth, should no more entitle a man to higher rewards than inherited wealth, rank, or skin color. It is this approach to equality that has been in the ascendant these last decades in the developed countries. It was given uncompromising expression in a recent book which has found a wide audience, *A Theory of Justice,* by the Harvard philosopher John Rawls.* Equality of opportunity is a delusion to Rawls, unless it produces equality of results, i.e., of incomes. This leads Rawls to conclude that what moral philosophers—and all major religions—have always considered "justice" is actually injustice, that is, rewards (and punishments) according to merit and performance. Justice consists, on the contrary, in giving compensation (Rawls calls it "redress") to those less equal in their condition, especially if the cause is a lack of "native assets," whether lack of ability or of motivation. Unlike most earlier advocates of total equality of condition, Rawls does not argue that *people* are inherently equal—quite the contrary. But he demands that *society* must be totally equal and should even favor the inherently less equal. Genetic disability may not be the fault of society; but inequality resulting therefrom is to Rawls a denial of justice and a social guilt.

This kind of equality, equality of income or of condition, is not primarily concerned with economic performance. Indeed, every advocate thereof has accepted a heavy economic cost as inevitable. Again the clearest statement of this is a recent one: *Equality and Efficiency, The Big Trade-off,* by Arthur M. Okun,† a highly respected economist and member of the Council of Economic Advisers under President Johnson. Okun professes himself a convinced egalitarian—in itself a novelty among economists who, almost without exception, consider equality of opportunity as being both more just and more efficacious. But Okun, while he "would like complete equality of income best of all," stresses that equality of condition has costs which equality of opportunity does not involve. Every advance

*(Cambridge, Mass.: Belknap Press, 1971).
†(Washington, D.C.: The Brookings Institute, 1975).

toward equality of income other than that resulting from greater equality of opportunity means a loss of efficiency and productivity. "Any insistence on carving the pie into equal slices would shrink the size of the pie." Hence an egalitarian policy must weigh the trade-offs between equality and efficiency; and society "can—indeed must—accept some measure of inequality of income as a 'practicality.'"

Equality of opportunity means "leveling up," though only gradually, not for all, and perhaps not even for a great many at any given time. Equality of condition, however, means "leveling down" for the majority.

Rawls and the root-and-branch egalitarians would no doubt reject as cravenly condoning "injustice" Okun's conclusion that a good deal of inequality of income must be accepted as "practicality"—just as Bakunin 100 years ago rejected Marx's similar argument. But not even Rawls would question Okun's premise that equality of income entails a cost in economic efficiency and productivity. He would only consider it irrelevant.

Neither Rawls nor Okun is saying anything that has not been said many times before, though both are saying it uncommonly well. What is new, however, is that no one in today's world argues publicly what was almost self-evident to earlier times: that inequality—whether based on rank, wealth, birth, priestly function, or learning as in a Confucian hierarchy—is proper, just, natural, and indeed necessary. No one today says with Shakespeare (in *Troilus and Cressida*):

> Oh, when Degree is shak'd,
> The Enterprise is sick.

On the contrary, popular rhetoric today would say:

> Unless Degree is shak'd,
> The Enterprise is sick.

The only argument is which approach to equality—whether through equality of opportunity or through equality of income and condition—is true "equality" and satisfies the demands of justice, equity, and morality.

But neither approach can be applied to the inequality of the population's new center of demographic gravity, the old people. We have to provide more equality of opportunity for older, retired people, not deny them the right to work as we now do. But this can only assuage the problem; it is no solution.

Implicit in the concept of "equality of opportunity" is the belief that once equal access has been provided, the individual will be able to become "equal" in condition and income. His inequality, whatever the cause, will disappear. This also implies that at least for the individual—though not perhaps for entire groups—"equality of opportunity" solves, indeed eliminates, the problem of "inequality." But even if we do away with mandatory retirement at any age, the inequality for the older people is only postponed, except for those who die.

How many of the older people would want to work, for how long, and in what jobs, we do not know. We do know that a great many are capable of working. In 1900, after all, a full third of the people who had held jobs before they reached age sixty-five continued to work beyond what is now "retirement age"—and their physical condition was far less good than that of the people reaching age sixty-five today, while their jobs were physically far more demanding. Today only one-seventh (14 percent) of former labor-force members work beyond age sixty-five—or at least report their earnings, which may not be quite the same thing considering the high Social Security penalties on earning more than a few pennies after age sixty-five. Surely in 1900 a great many who worked would have preferred to retire had they been financially able. Today, on the contrary, many who do not work would prefer to do so if permitted under Social Security regulations and if not shut out by compulsory retirement at a fixed age. Among manual workers there are indeed many who do not miss the job, or the companionship or the stimulus. All they miss when they retire is the paycheck. But for professional, managerial, technical people on all levels, and for skilled workers and craftsmen, retirement, even with adequate income, is a threat rather than something to look forward to.

But even if labor-force participation of those over sixty-five were to exceed the 1900 figure of one third for those in their mid and late sixties—and this is quite possible—the figure for people still at work in their seventies, eighties, or nineties would surely be much smaller. People who work and perform at a very advanced age are, of course, by no means unknown—Casals, Picasso, Mr. Justice Holmes, and Toscanini are recent examples. But the great majority, even if physical strength permits, are unlikely to muster the inner resources and the motivation which keep the artist, the writer, the scholar, or the entrepreneur working into advanced years. And the greatest increase in older people from now on is going to result from longevity rather than from an increase in the numbers of people who reach age sixty-five. It is also among the older age groups—with retirement benefits reduced as their spouse dies, with savings likely to be used up, suffering from increased loneliness, and in greater need of health care—that the inequality under which they live becomes greatest and bites the most deeply.

The inequality of the older, retired people is therefore at least in larger part inequality of condition rather than of opportunity. And the "condition" itself is irreversible. It is inequality because of a "lack of native assets," to use Rawls's euphemism.

But the only way to make the incomes of the older people more equal, indeed the only way to prevent their incomes from becoming even less equal, is greater "efficiency." Any "trade-off" between equality and efficiency can only make their inequality greater. In that respect the situation of the old people differs fundamentally from that of any other "disadvantaged" group: "leveling down" can only be at their expense, never to their benefit. To increase their equality at the cost of sacrificing "efficiency" is economically untenable and politically impossible. It would also be morally wrong, even for the most committed egalitarian, e.g., a John Rawls.

One reason is the size of the need. Even to maintain the older, retired people in their present state of relative inequality will require a massive increase in productivity. In numbers they will grow by as much as the work force will grow; even if the barriers to their equality of access and of opportunity are lowered—that is, if the penalties on their keeping on in work are lowered or removed—the dependency ratio can at best only be prevented from deteriorating further. Measures to promote the equality of income of the older people at the expense of "efficiency," that is, of productivity, can therefore only decrease the share of the national income available for the support of the older, retired people—either, as would be most likely, through inflation or through cuts in their retirement stipends.

Politically too, it seems most unlikely (if not impossible) to increase the amounts available to the older, retired people by making smaller the "slice of the pie" that goes to the working population. The employed people these last twenty years have shown that they will only accept higher charges for pensions, whether in the form of higher Social Security taxes or of higher payments into private pension plans, if their own cash income goes up by the same amount. And the employed people are the only ones who can finance higher real incomes for the retired people. No other pool of income or of wealth is available. Egalitarian rhetoric always assumes that the "inequality of condition" is caused by some other group's "profiteering"; it is caused by the "privileged," the "advantaged," the "fat cats." But the inequality of the older, retired people is not caused by anyone's profiteering. There is no "wrong" to be "redressed." No one gets the youth which is lost in the aging process. And the employees of America would hardly be receptive to the argument that they are the "privileged" and the "profiteers." Politically, the only way to make greater equality for the older, retired people acceptable at all is by increasing the size of the pie rather than increasing the size of the slice at the expense of shrinking the pie—in other words, at the expense of "efficiency."

Morally, too, the standard egalitarian argument does not make sense when applied to the inequality of income of older, retired people. The "cost" of greater equality for these people if achieved through a "trade-off" between efficiency and equality would be fully borne by the very same people who benefit, except that everybody all around would get less. For the group that would be asked to give up something are those same people who, in a few years or, at most, a few decades, will be old and retired themselves. Such a sacrifice could be morally justified only if it provided permanent, or anyway long-term, "redress" for the unequal condition of a group; not if it in the long term creates greater inequality.

Further, the "trade-off" between equality and efficiency as an approach to the inequality of condition of the older, retired population is not only economically impractical and politically unacceptable. It lacks moral justification. What is needed—economically, politically, and morally—is more income all around, which means greater "efficiency" all around. This normally calls for emphasis on "equality of opportunity" rather than on "equality of income." But in the case of the older people, greater "equality of opportunity" only assuages, only postpones. We therefore have to develop an approach to "equality of income" that considers the "trade-off" between equality and efficiency as inimical to equality and yet stresses greater equality of income. To fall back on the traditional response to the egalitarian, that "equality of opportunity" will take care of most of the problem, will not do in the case of the older, retired people. But the traditional "egalitarianism" itself will do even less.

We may therefore see the emergence of two kinds of "egalitarianism," both pressing for "equality of income" rather than "equality of opportunity," but in opposition on the means through which each hopes to obtain its greater equality. The traditional "disadvantaged" groups—the very poor or the disadvantaged blacks in American society, for instance—will continue to press for equality at the cost of efficiency, e.g., through "reverse discrimination" which provides economic security, jobs, promotions, and income as "redress" either for past deprivations or, in Professor Rawls's terms, because they have "fewer native assets" or were "born into less favorable social positions." The new "disadvantaged" group, the older, retired people, do not want "redress"; they need greater equality on the basis of greater efficiency.

In fact, this development may actually be well under way. Nothing hurt Senator George McGovern quite as much in his unsuccessful bid for the American presidency in 1972 as his attempts to win support from the vocal "egalitarians," which however cost him the support of the workers, and especially of the older and supposedly "class-conscious" blue-collar workers. "The hardhats are reactionaries," was the standard, "liberal" explanation. But in the comments reported in the press during the campaign, the older workers were quoted again and again as explaining their rejection of McGovern in such words as: "I have to think of my retirement pension and his proposals endanger it." They were perhaps no less "egalitarian" than McGovern. But their concern was with the new need for equality of income and condition for the older, retired people (i.e., for themselves a few years out) rather than with the traditional egalitarian needs. And they spoke for a far larger "disadvantaged minority" than the ones to which McGovern tried to appeal.

Equality versus equality therefore may well become a central issue under pension fund socialism—with an equality based on greater "efficiency" and an equality based on "redress" leading to very different policies and to sharp cleavages between the two groups.

There is no complete or clean solution in sight. The issue is one of "right" against "right," on which even compromises are difficult. But it is most unlikely that it can be postponed for very long, let alone avoided altogether, whether in the United States or any other developed country. There is just not enough economic product available to satisfy both demands for "equality." The real question will be how much is left for the "disadvantaged" and for "redress," and how much "efficiency" society and economy will be willing to sacrifice for their satisfaction. For in economics, in politics—and perhaps even in conscience—the demands of the older people, that is, the demands that can only be satisfied through greater "efficiency," will surely predominate.

**Inflation versus Unemployment:
Which Is the Lesser Evil?**

Ever since the Great Depression, unemployment has been seen as both the endemic and the most dangerous disease of modern society and economy. Under pension fund socialism, inflation can be expected to take over both roles instead. The question whether unemployment becomes the lesser evil, and just how much unemployment a society can and will accept in order to control inflation, can then be expected to become a central political issue.

Pension fund socialism and the demographic changes underlying it make the economy prone to inflation in two ways. One, of course, is the attempt to increase both the employed worker's wage and the employer's pension contributions (or the retired worker's pension), without a corresponding increase in total productivity. And since the employed worker will not accept a higher Social Security or pension contribution without an offsetting increase in his wage income, that danger is always present.

The second danger of inflation stems from the steady transfer of "savings" into "pseudo-savings," that is, into the consumption of the retired people. Unless this is offset by an increase in real capital formation, it must result in what the British have come to call "stagflation": economic stagnation for lack of capital investment, accompanied by inflationary consumption pressures on prices.

Inflation is the greatest threat to the retired people on pensions, and an equally great one to the workers over fifty with an increasing stake in the future purchasing power of their retirement benefits. Together, these two groups constitute a near-majority of the adult population; by 1985 they will constitute an actual majority. These two groups, as a result of pension fund socialism, have a far greater interest in preventing inflation than ever existed before. A substantial constituency of this kind, sharing a common concern, is by definition a major "interest group" in the American political system and a potent political force.

Continuing inflation, even at a low rate (say 2 or 3 percent a year) erodes the value of the provisions for retirement. A 3 percent inflation rate halves the value of the average pension dollar, that is, the dollar which a worker in his early forties puts in to get retirement benefits at age sixty-five. Double-digit inflation actually destroys a pension fund within a few short years. Provisions for the future are meaningful only if the purchasing power of money can be assumed to be reasonably stable. Not only would inflation erode the value of pension provisions made for the future, it would erode, if not destroy, the value and meaning of pensions for the people at work and their willingness to give up current purchasing power in order to have security in the future.

We have known for a long time that inflation is a corrosive social poison, dissolving the bonds of trust in community and society. Every inflation for 400 years has resulted in alienation of the very class on which society depends: the "middle class," those people who carry the values, the institutions, the productive (and not only the economically productive) resources of the community; and who, on the other hand, have just enough economic substance to get by. Inflation for these people is a danger to their social position, to their self-respect, and to their belief in the equity of society and community. Economists, however, especially these last thirty years, have tended to laugh off inflation as an economic problem, if not to proclaim that a little inflation is a permanent good.* But as the pension

*It should be said that there is not the slightest evidence for the belief, popular among "liberal" economists these last thirty years, that a "little inflation" means

trust becomes the means to organize economic performance for social needs, inflation can no longer even be defended economically. Even a "little inflation," an inflation
at rates which "liberal" economists would consider minimal, is a threat to the retired and to those who are past early
middle age.

At the same time—and this is quite novel—unemployment is far less of a threat, if a threat at all, for the "constituency" of the pension funds, i.e., retired people and
older workers. Obviously the people who are already
retired are not threatened directly (nor very much even
indirectly) by unemployment. Older workers over fifty who
have enough seniority to have substantial protection in a
layoff, and who already have a heavy stake in retirement
benefits, might see their interest in similar terms. This may
explain why in the 1973–75 recession inflation rather than
unemployment remained the greatest concern of the voters, despite high unemployment figures, and why the "folks
back home" could not be roused to enthusiasm for anti-
recession and anti-deflation measures espoused by their
own union leaders and the "liberals" they had elected to
the Congress.

Economic policy should be able to attain both steady
employment and a stable currency. Indeed, as recently as
the Eisenhower years this was taken for granted. The
demographics of pension fund socialism should make it
easier to attain high and steady employment for all groups
—excepting only minority teenagers, for whom no policy

---

good times and economic growth. The well-documented relationship between
price movements, employment, and standard of living for the 350 years between
the great inflation of the sixteenth century and the outbreak of World War II and
since, would argue that there is no correlation, if it does not support the conten-
tion that periods of stable (if not slowly falling) prices are the most prosperous
times, easiest for the masses and conducive to economic growth.

whatever will be able to provide jobs in adequate numbers, let alone of quality, for a decade to come or more. The demographics as well as the economics of pension fund socialism will, however, make it more difficult to prevent inflation than it was twenty years ago.

Under the age and occupational structure with which the United States will live the next twenty-five years, to the end of this century, a policy of high employment and stable dollar value would require:

A steady, sustained rise in the productivity of all key resources, and above all, of capital and of knowledge workers;

a steady sustained rise in capital formation, that is, willingness to put a larger share of increasing incomes into savings rather than consumption; and

an end to the upward trend in the share of public expenditures and national incomes that goes to "transfer payments" and welfare expenditures—even though expenditures to support the older, retired people will inexorably take a larger share of both public expenditures and national income. Other welfare expenditures, in other words, would have to go down fairly sharply at least as a proportion of national income.

Even in terms of economics alone these are demanding requirements, though by no means impossible ones. Politically, they obviously would be highly unpopular today. But if these requirements are not met, a choice will have to be made. *What is the lesser cost:* unemployment, even at a fairly high level, or inflation?

Economists and politicians would tend, as a whole, to consider inflation the lesser evil and one that is "controllable." But are the voters under pension fund socialism still likely to agree?

5. New Alignments in American Politics

We have seen that pension fund socialism and the demographic changes underlying it will create new problems and demand new policies. They will create new issues and, predictably, make irrelevant many of the most visible issues of the last generation. They will fundamentally affect the temper, mood, values, and behavior of American society and, with it, of American politics.

We have also seen that pension fund socialism is in the process of creating a genuine new "interest group." And through the pension funds, it is creating the institutions around which this interest group can organize, institutions which represent the concerns and priorities of the new center of population and social gravity: older people on retirement and the older employees (past fifty or so) to whom retirement provisions are becoming increasingly important.

But will this new interest group lead also to a realignment in American politics? It has all the qualifications to become a new political center. It is an interest group which cuts across existing lines. It contains whites and blacks, men and women, the middle class, the white-collar worker, and the blue-collar worker. It is thus capable of integrating people from all areas of American society and of mobilizing them for joint action in a common interest. It is a group with clearly definable interests; yet these are not divisive but integrating, interests—such as enable people, otherwise separated by their sectional concerns, to join in common effort. It could thus serve as a unifying focus, the center of American politics.

It is, further, a group with clearly defined self-interests. But they are not "selfish" interests. "What is good for the older people is good for America," may not be the "sexiest" slogan, but it is a plausible one. As an interest group, the new population center of gravity could therefore present itself as acting in the best interests of the entire society. After all, almost every adult member of this society—certainly the great majority who are employed and working—sees himself eventually as a member of the new group. What is good for it may not be good for him right away; but it is also not inimical to his own long-term interests. "Long-term" means, after all, only a few years for the large and growing segment of the working population that has already reached the age where its retirement support is a major concern, and the pension claim by far its largest asset and most valuable property.

An effective political faction requires common, identifiable "enemies," and the new group has such "enemies." There are three major issues on which the new interest group is held together by common opposition. These issues are, first, the interests of the "welfare society" of the retirement and pension system against the "welfare state"; second, the interest in productivity to redress its own inequality versus those egalitarian demands that threaten productivity; and third, the interest in a stable currency as one priority, if not the first priority, of economic policy. Beyond this, however, the new interest group has no "do's" or "don'ts." It is flexible and can work with anybody else. By and large, its imperatives do not put it into conflict with the traditional major interest groups of American society—whether labor, the farmer, business, or the employed middle class.

This new interest group has its own representative institution: the pension fund. Therefore, it has the means to organize itself for visibility, representation, and action. It has the organ through which it can make effective the controlling ownership in American business which it already holds. It has a "professional" representative in the "asset manager" and therefore access to the universities, the journalists, the opinion-makers, let alone the politicians. And the fact that this organ is quite different from the traditional organizations through which American interest groups have reached such opinion-makers and decision-makers may actually make it more effective and more powerful. The "asset manager," precisely because he is a professional, is not a lobbyist.

Finally, this new group is permanent. Both in numbers, that is, in absolute strength, and in the proportion of the adult population, that is, in relative strength, it will grow for a long time to come. The "youth generation" of the sixties was also a new "demographic center of gravity," to be sure. But at the very time when it became visible, vocal, and influential, it was already a transient, short-lived phenomenon and declining. And unlike "disadvantaged minority groups" the older people are not held together by a condition which either individual success or social action can change and make unimportant. The condition of the older people as well as their numerical weight are permanent, or at least "givens" for long decades to come.

These are almost the ideal, textbook qualifications for an interest group in America to become the center of political alignments. And pension fund socialism has emerged just at the time when the traditional alignments of American politics seem to be in utter confusion and disarray. Will this new interest group representing pension fund socialism bring about a major realignment in American politics? Will it become the new center, the new "majority"?

It certainly cannot be ruled out that pension fund socialism will lead to the emergence of a permanent majority— though not the "silent majority" nor the "new majority" nor any of the other "majorities" which have been talked about these last few years. This permanent majority would comprise the employees over fifty or fifty-five, or that majority among them that is under employer pension plans; the self-employed with their own rapidly growing pension plans, which would include such potent groups as the lawyers, the physicians, the small businessmen, and the productive family farmers; the retired employees under pension plans; and the managements of institutions with private pension plans which, in addition to business, would include the health care institutions and a goodly part of the country's educational institutions, but also governments, especially local governments, whose solvency is threatened by inflationary pressures on pension plan funding.

This, in many ways, would be a reconstitution of the "old majority," that majority of farmer, skilled labor, and small business which Mark Hanna built in the 1890s and which dominated the country until the rise of mass production and giant corporations, the depression and the advent of the New Deal.

Mark Hanna's majority of 1896 is considered today to have been conservative, if not reactionary. This was not how his contemporaries saw it, including Samuel Gompers, the founder of the American Federation of Labor. Indeed, Mark Hanna's majority was basically a radical one. It put a new principle in the center and established it as foundation for the common interest. Mark Hanna no longer believed in the "invisible hand" of self-interest; but he still believed in an "invisible hand": productivity, tested in the market. It was productivity which established the common focus of interest for the major groups in Mark Hanna's America. It was productivity that drove Mark Hanna's economic engine. This was radical innovation in 1896. Indeed, the very word "productivity" was coined in Mark Hanna's circle, if not by Mark Hanna himself, as a manifesto to oust from power the old conservatives who had controlled the Republican Party ever since the Civil War, and whose majority was rapidly crumbling. But while Mark Hanna's new "invisible hand" established his new majority in power and gave it cohesion for more than a generation, it, in the last analysis, became his undoing during the Great Depression.*

A new permanent majority would have "a visible hand": the pension fund mechanism, which both symbolizes and makes effective the direct relationship between economic performance and economic welfare. This majority would have a great many internal conflicts—but so did Mark Hanna's majority of farmer, skilled worker, and small business. It would, however, also have major common interests, in economic performance, in equality based on efficiency, and in the stability of the currency. It would have what every permanent political grouping needs: common enemies—

*Very few people seem to know that Mark Hanna not only founded the National Association of Manufacturers, but also played a crucial role in the formation of the American Federation of Labor (second perhaps only to Samuel Gompers) and was largely responsible for the development of "business unionism." It was this national interest in economic performance and high wages that Mark Hanna meant by the term "free enterprise," which he in all likelihood coined to distinguish the "American system" from "capitalism."

the "bureaucracy" and "transfer payments" to those not contributing from their earnings to the majority's pension funds and retirement monies but expecting to be supported by them. It would thus be able to develop both a political platform and an economic program.

This would not be a "conservative" majority. In fact, in many ways it would have a strong tendency toward radicalism, for example, in health care, housing, and equal rights for women. But the issues it would see as crucial—the emotions it feels, the things it considers important—would be very different from those which are seen, felt, and considered important today by "liberals" and "conservatives" alike. And the questions it will ask are almost certain to be totally different. In other words this alignment, if it comes, will be genuinely "new." It will no more bear resemblance to the conservative alignment of pre-New Deal days than to the liberal alignment of the last forty years.

Today such a majority might seem quite unlikely. But it is no more unlikely than Mark Hanna's "majority"—the majority that brought the Republican Party to power in 1896 and held together after that for thirty-five years— must have seemed to the conventional wisdom at the time of Cleveland, of Bryan, or of the traditional Republicans of the "GOP" of 1890. This new majority would require great political leadership. But it might also be brought together by the demagogue railing against "pointy-headed bureaucrats."

Predicting a new alignment for American politics is one of our oldest political sports. Since the earliest days of the Republic, every political alignment and every "majority" has appeared precarious, fragile, in disarray, on the point of unraveling. Yet such alignments, once established, have shown tremendous staying power in American politics. They have changed far less often than in any other country

—perhaps because they are non-ideological and unashamedly interest-based. Existing political alignments in the United States are singularly resistant to political theory. Not only do they survive defeats; unlike most coalitions, whether political or military, American political alignments even survive their victories.

But realignments do occur. What tends to bring them about are fundamental changes in the population structure and in the center of population gravity. American political alignments change, as a rule, when new major institutions emerge as the result of fundamental shifts in the structure of ownership and in the control of major productive resources. What triggers realignment in American politics is thus precisely the kind of development which constitutes "the unseen revolution," the kind of development that brought pension fund socialism to America.

The emergence of the pension funds, therefore, offers the possibility—for the first time perhaps since the 1930s —of a genuine realignment in American politics, a realignment based on the realization that America has achieved her own distinct brand of "socialism."

1995 Epilogue: The Governance of Corporations

Fifteen years after it was first chronicled, the "unseen revolution" transforming corporate ownership in the United States is now visible to all. The 20 largest pension funds (13 of them funds of state, municipal, or nonprofit employees) hold around one-tenth of the equity capital of America's publicly owned companies. All told, institutional investors—that is, primarily pension funds—control close to 40 percent of the common stock of the country's large (and many midsize) businesses. The largest and fastest-growing funds, those of public employees, are no longer content to be passive investors. Increasingly, they demand a voice in the companies in which they invest—for instance, a veto over board appointments, executive compensation, and critical corporate charter provisions.

Equally important, and still largely overlooked, pension funds also hold 40 percent or so of the medium-term and long-term debt of the country's bigger companies. Thus, these institutions have become corporate America's largest lenders as well as its largest owners. As the finance texts have stressed for years, the power of the lender is as great as the power of the owner—sometimes greater.

* This epilogue was first published in the *Harvard Business Review* (March-April 1991).

The rise of pension funds as dominant owners and lenders represents one of the most startling power shifts in economic history. The first modern pension fund was established in 1950 by General Motors. Four decades later, pension funds control total assets of $2.5 trillion, divided about equally between common stocks and fixed-income securities. Demographics guarantee that these assets will grow aggressively for at least another ten years. Barring a prolonged depression, pension funds will have to invest $100 billion to $200 billion in new resources every year throughout the 1990s.

America's failure, until quite recently, to recognize (let alone address) this power shift accounts in large measure for much of the financial turbulence of the 1980s—the hostile takeovers, the leveraged buyouts, and the general restructuring frenzy. Two problems in particular demand attention: For what should America's new owners, the pension funds, hold corporate management accountable? And what is the appropriate institutional structure through which to exercise accountability?

Actually, the United States is quite late among developed countries in concentrating ownership of large companies in a small number of institutions. In Germany, the country's three major banks have long controlled around 60 percent of the share capital of the larger companies, partly through direct holdings, partly through the holdings of their customers that, under German law, the banks manage and vote on. In Japan, the majority of large companies are members of a small number (ten at most) of industrial groups, the now familiar *keiretsu*. In a keiretsu, 20 percent to 30 percent of the share capital of each member company is held by the other members and by the group's bank and trading company, and practically all credit to the member companies is provided by the group's bank. In Italy, half of the country's large businesses have been owned or controlled by the state since the 1930s.

(IRI, the biggest state holding company, is the second-largest company in all of Europe.) The rest of Italy's big businesses are under the control of five or six huge conglomerates such as the Fiat Group.

Ownership in the United States is quite different. It is indeed unique. In Europe and Japan, stock ownership is a means to nonfinancial ends. A German bank's income from the companies to which it is the *hausbank* comes through commercial relationships rather than through its ownership stake. Deutsche Bank, Germany's largest financial institution, gets many times as much in fees from client companies for mundane services such as letters of credit as it receives from them in stock dividends. The keiretsu's first concern is power—power in the market, power over suppliers and subcontractors, power and influence with ministries and civil servants. As for tangible benefits, a keiretsu company profits far more from the business it gets from the other members than from their dividends. The government holdings in Italy constitute the largest concentration of economic power in any market economy. They serve primarily political objectives. The companies are run to provide jobs in politically important regions, to create lucrative executive positions for the party faithful, and to supply campaign funds for the parties in power.

Neither the German banks nor the Japanese keiretsu nor Italy's government nor its conglomerates have much interest in share prices or capital gains. They do not intend to sell. The American pension fund, by contrast, has no commercial ties to the companies in which it invests or to which it lends. It is not a "business" at all but an "asset manager." There are, as we shall see, important lessons to be learned from developments in Europe and in Japan, both as to what to do and what not to do. But in the United States, the rapid shift of ownership and credit power to these new and quite different owners poses totally new and very different problems.

Pension funds first emerged as the premier owners of the country's share capital in the early 1970s. But for 15 or 20 years thereafter, the realities of pension fund ownership were ignored. In part this was because the pension funds themselves did not want to be "owners." They wanted to be passive "investors" and short-term investors at that. "We do not buy a company," they asserted. "We buy shares that we sell as soon as they no longer offer good prospects for capital gains over a fairly short time." Moreover, the development was totally at variance with American tradition and with what everybody took for granted—and many still take for granted—as the structure of the U.S. economy. Long after pension funds had become the largest holders of equity capital, the United States was still referred to as the country of "people's capitalism" in which millions of individuals each owned small pieces of the country's large companies. To be sure, employees have become the owners of America's means of production. But their ownership is exercised through a fairly small number of very large "trustees."

Finally, though, the fog has begun to lift. The trustees of pension funds, especially those representing public employees, are waking up to the fact that they are no longer investors in shares. An investor, by definition, can sell holdings. A small pension fund may still be able to do so. There are thousands of such small funds, but their total holdings represent no more than a quarter or so of all pension fund assets. The share holdings of even a midsize pension fund are already so large that they are not easily sold. Or more precisely, these holdings can, as a rule, be sold only if another pension fund buys them. They are much too large to be easily absorbed by the retail market and are thus permanently part of the circular trading among institutions.

Ownership in the United States is far less concentrated than in Germany, Japan, or Italy—and will remain far less concentrated. Hence, the U.S. pension fund still has more elbow room than the big bank in Germany, the keiretsu in Japan, or the industrial conglomerate in Italy. But some large U.S. pension funds each own as much as 1 percent or even 2 percent of a big company's total capital. All pension funds together may own 35 percent of the company's total capital. (For example, pension funds own 75 percent of the equity of the Chase Manhattan Bank.) The 1 percent holder cannot sell easily. And the 40 percent holder, that is, the pension fund community at large, cannot sell at all. It is almost as committed as the German hausbank to a client company or the Japanese keiretsu to a member company. Thus, the large funds are beginning to learn what Georg Siemens, founder of Deutsche Bank and inventor of the hausbank system, said a hundred years ago when he was criticized for spending so much of his and the bank's time on a troubled client company: "If one can't sell, one must care."

Pension funds cannot be managers as were so many nineteenth-century owners. Yet a business, even a small one, needs strong, autonomous management with the authority, continuity, and competence to build and run the organization. Thus, pension funds, as America's new owners, will increasingly have to make sure that a company has the management it needs. As we have learned over the last 40 years, this means that management must be clearly accountable to somebody and that accountability must be institutionally anchored. It means that management must be accountable for *performance* and *results* rather than for good intentions, however beautifully quantified. It means that accountability must involve financial accountability, even though everyone knows that performance and results go way beyond the financial "bottom line."

Surely, most people will say, we know what performance and results mean for business enterprise. We should, of course, because clearly defining these terms is a prerequisite both for effective management and for successful and profitable ownership. In fact, there have been two definitions offered in the 40 years since World War II. Neither has stood the test of time.

The first definition was formulated around 1950, at about the same time at which the modern pension fund was invented. The most prominent of the period's "professional managers," Ralph Cordiner, CEO of the General Electric Company, asserted that top management in the large, publicly owned corporation was a "trustee." Cordiner argued that senior executives were responsible for managing the enterprise "in the best-balanced interest of shareholders, customers, employees, suppliers, and plant community cities. " That is, what we now call "stakeholders."

Cordiner's answer, as some of us pointed out right away, still required a clear definition of results and of the meaning of "best" with respect to "balance." It also required a clear structure of accountability with an independent and powerful organ of supervision and control to hold management accountable for performance and results. Otherwise, professional management becomes an enlightened despot—and enlightened despots, whether platonic philosopher kings or CEOs, neither perform nor last.

But Cordiner's generation and its executive successors did not define what performance and results produce the best balance, nor did they develop any kind of accountability. As a result, professional management, 1950s-style, has neither performed nor lasted.

The single most powerful blow to Cordiner-style management was the rise of the hostile takeover in the late 1970s. One after the other of such managers has been toppled. The survivors have been forced to change drastically how they manage or at least to change their rhetoric. No top management I know now claims to run its business as a "trustee" for the "best-balanced interests" of "stakeholders."

Pension funds have been the driving force behind this change. Without the concentration of voting power in a few pension funds and the funds' willingness to endorse hostile transactions, most of the raiders' attacks would never have been launched. A raider who has to get support from millions of dispersed individual stockholders soon runs out of time and money.

To be sure, pension fund managers had serious doubts about many buyouts and takeovers, about their impact on the companies in play, and about their value to the economy. Pension fund managers—especially the moderately paid civil servants running the funds of public employees—also had serious aesthetic and moral misgivings about such things as "greenmail" and the huge fortunes earned by corporate raiders, lawyers, and investment bankers. Yet they felt they had no choice but to provide money for takeovers and buyouts and to tender their shares into them. They did so in droves.

One reason for their support was that these transactions kept alive the illusion that pension funds could in fact sell their shares—that is, that they were "investors" still. Takeovers and LBOs also offered immediate capital gains. And since pension fund portfolios have by and large done quite poorly, such gains were most welcome—though, as will be discussed shortly, they too were more illusion than reality.

What made takeovers and buyouts inevitable (or at least created the opportunity for them) was the mediocre performance of enlightened-despot management, the management without clear definitions of performance and results and with no clear accountability to somebody. It may be argued that the mediocre performance of so many of America's large corporations in the last 30 years was not management's fault, that it resulted instead from wrong-headed public policies that have kept American savings rates low and capital costs high. But captains are responsible for what happens on their watches. And whatever the reasons or excuses, the large U.S company has not done particularly well on professional management's watch—whether measured by competitiveness, market standing, or innovative performance. As for financial performance, it has, by and large, not even earned the minimum acceptable result, a return on equity equal to its cost of capital.

The raiders thus performed a needed function. As an old proverb has it, "If there are no grave diggers, one needs vultures." But takeovers and buyouts are very radical surgery. And even if radical surgery is not life-threatening, it inflicts profound shock. Takeovers and buyouts deeply disturb and indeed alienate middle managers and professionals, the very people on whose motivation, effort, and loyalty a business depends. For these people, the takeover or dismantling of a company to which they have given years of service is nothing short of betrayal. It is a denial of all they must believe in to work productively and with devotion. As a result, few of the companies that were taken over or sold in a buyout performed any better a few years later than they had performed under the old dispensation.

But weren't takeovers and buyouts at least good for shareholders? Perhaps not. In a typical transaction, shareholders (and this means primarily the pension funds) received, say, $60 for a share that had been quoted on the stock exchange for an average of $40 in the year before the deal. This 50 percent premium is proving to have been an illusion in many cases. Perhaps $25 of the $60 was not solid cash but the value put by the raider or the raider's investment banker on convertible warrants, unsecured loans, or junk bonds. These noncash nonsecurities, which were bought by many of the same institutions that sold shares, are rapidly losing value.

Many pension funds immediately did sell these now-depreciating pieces of paper. But they sold them to other pension funds or institutional investors—there are no other buyers. Thus, the net financial value of these transactions to the pension fund community at large remains suspect indeed.

Today nearly all CEOs of large U.S. companies proclaim that they run their enterprises "in the interest of the shareholders" and "to maximize shareholder value." This is the second definition of performance and results developed over the past 40 years. It sounds much less noble than Cordiner's assertion of the "best-balanced interest," but it also sounds much more realistic. Yet its life span will be even shorter than yesterday's professional management. For most people, "maximizing shareholder value" means a higher share price within six months or a year—certainly not much longer. Such short-term capital gains are the wrong objective for both the enterprise and its dominant shareholders. As a theory of corporate performance, then, "maximizing shareholder value" has little staying power.

Regarding the enterprise, the cost of short-term thinking hardly needs to be argued. But short-term capital gains are also of no benefit to holders who cannot sell. The interest of a large pension fund is in the value of a holding at the time at which a beneficiary turns from being an employee who pays into the fund into a pensioner who gets paid by the fund. Concretely, this means that the time over which a fund invests—the time until its future beneficiaries will retire—is on average 15 years rather than 3 months or 6 months. This is the appropriate return horizon for these owners.

There is, however, one group that does—or at least thinks it does—have an interest in short-term gains. These are the employers with "defined benefit" pension plans. Until now, in a classic case of the tail wagging the dog, the interests of these employers have dominated how the pension fund community approaches its role as owner. In a defined-benefit plan, retiring employees receive fixed annual payments, usually a percentage of their wages during the last three or five years on the job. The employer's annual contribution fluctuates with the value of the fund's assets. If in any given year that value is high (compared with the amount needed on an actuarial basis to cover the fund's future pension obligations) the employer's contribution is cut. If the fund's asset value is low, the contribution goes up.

We owe the defined-benefit trust to mere accident. When General Motors management proposed the pension fund in 1950, several powerful board members resisted it as a giveaway to the union. The directors relented only when promised that, under a defined-benefit plan, the company would have to pay little or nothing. An ever-rising stock market, so the argument went, would create the assets needed to pay future pensions. Most private employers followed the GM model, if only because they too deluded themselves into believing that the stock market rather than the company would take care of the pension obligation.

Needless to say, this was wishful thinking. Most defined-benefit plans have done poorly, precisely because they have been chasing inappropriate short-term gains. The other kind of plan, the "defined contribution" plan under which the employer contributes each year a defined percentage of the employee's annual salary or wages, has done better in a good many cases. Indeed, defined-benefit plans are rapidly losing their allure. Because they have not delivered the promised capital gains, a great many are seriously underfunded. From now on, as a result of new accounting standards, such underfunding has to be shown as a liability on the employing company's balance sheet. This means that even in a mild recession (in which both a company's earnings and the stock market are down), a good many companies will actually be pushed to, if not over, the brink of insolvency. And what many of them have done in good years—that is, to siphon off the actuarial surplus in the pension fund and show it as "net income" in their income statement—is unlikely to be permitted much longer.

Company after company is therefore going out of defined-benefit plans. By the end of the decade, they will have become marginal. As a result, short-term gains as an objective for the major owners of American business will no longer dominate. They are already playing second fiddle. Public-employee funds are defined-contribution plans, and they constitute the majority of the biggest funds. Being independent of corporate management, they, rather than the pension funds of private businesses, are taking the lead and writing the new script.

We no longer need to theorize about how to define performance and results in the large enterprise. We have successful examples. Both the Germans and the Japanese have highly concentrated institutional ownership. In neither country can the owners actually manage. In both countries industry has done extremely well in the 40 years since its near destruction in World War II. It has done well in terms of the overall economy of its country. It has also done exceedingly well for its shareholders. Whether invested in 1950, 1960, 1970, or 1980, $100,000 put into something like an index fund in the stock exchanges of Tokyo or Frankfurt would today be worth a good deal more than a similar investment in a New York Stock Exchange index fund.

How, then, do the institutional owners of German or Japanese industry define performance and results? Though they manage quite differently, they define them in the same way. Unlike Cordiner, they do not "balance" anything. They maximize. But they do not attempt to maximize shareholder value or the short-term interest of any one of the enterprise's "stakeholders." Rather, they *maximize the wealth-producing capacity of the enterprise.*[1] It is this objective that integrates short-term and long-term results and that ties the operational dimensions of business performance—market standing, innovation, productivity, and people and their development—with financial needs and financial results. It is also this objective on which all constituencies depend for the satisfaction of their expectations and objectives, whether shareholders, customers, or employees.

To define performance and results as "maximizing the wealth-producing capacity of the enterprise" may be criticized as vague. To be sure, one doesn't get the answers by filling out forms. Decisions need to be made, and economic decisions that commit scarce resources to an uncertain future are always risky and controversial. When Ralph Cordiner first attempted to define performance and results—no one had tried to do so earlier—maximizing the wealth-producing capacity of the enterprise would indeed have been pretty fuzzy. By now, after four decades of work by many people, it has become crisp. All the elements that go into the process can be quantified with considerable rigor and are indeed quantified by those archquantifiers, by the planning departments of large Japanese companies and by many of the German companies as well.

The first step toward a clear definition of the concept was probably taken in my 1954 book, *The Practice of Management,* which outlined eight key objective areas for a business. These areas (or some variations thereof) are still the starting point for business planning in the large Japanese company. Since then, management analysts have done an enormous amount of work on the strategy needed to convert objectives into performance, including the pioneering work of Harvard Business School's Michael Porter and important new concepts such as "core competence" developed in HBR by C.K. Prahalad and Gary Hamel.[2]

Financial objectives are needed to tie all this together. Indeed, financial accountability is the key to the performance of management and enterprise. Without financial accountability, there is no accountability at all. And without financial accountability, there will also be no results in any other area. It is commonly believed in the United States that the Japanese are not profit conscious. This is simply not true. In fact, their profitability goals as measured against the cost of capital tend to be a good deal higher than those of most American companies. Only the Japanese do not start with profitability; they end with it.

Finally, maximizing the wealth-producing capacity of the enterprise also helps define the roles of institutional owners and their relationship to the enterprise. German and Japanese management structure and style differ greatly. But institutional owners in both countries support a management regardless of short-term results as long as the company performs according to a business plan that is designed to maximize the enterprise's wealth-producing capacity—and that is agreed upon between management and whatever organ represents the owners. This makes both sides focus on results. It makes management accountable. But it gives a performing company's management the needed continuity and security.

What we have is not the "final answer." Still, it is no longer theory but proven practice. And its results, to judge by German and Japanese business performance, are clearly superior to running the enterprise as a "trustee" for stakeholders or to maximize short-term gains for shareholders.

The one thing that we in the United States have yet to work out—and we have to work out ourselves—is how to build the new definition of management accountability into an institutional structure. We need what a political scientist would call a constitution—provisions that spell out, as does the German company law, the duties and responsibilities of management and that clarify the respective rights of other groups, especially the shareholders. *What* we have to do the Germans and the Japanese can show us. *How* we do it will have to be quite different to fit U.S. conditions.

In both Germany and Japan, managements are supervised closely and judged carefully. In Germany, a senior executive of the hausbank sits on the board of each company in which the bank has substantial holdings, usually as chairperson of the supervisory board. The bank's representative is expected to move fast whenever management fails to perform to exacting standards. In Japan, the chief executives of the major companies in a keiretsu—headed either by the CEO of the group's bank or by the CEO of the group's trading company—function as the executive committee of the whole group. They meet regularly. The top executives of the Mitsubishi group, for instance, meet every other Friday for three or four hours. They carefully review the business plans of each group's companies and evaluate the performance of each group's managements. Again and again, though usually without fanfare, chief executives who are found wanting are moved out, kicked upstairs, or shifted to the sidelines.

The analysis and scrutiny of management's performance is organized as systematic work in both countries. In Germany, it is done by the *sekretariat* of the big banks—invented in the 1870s by Deutsche Bank, which modeled it on the Prussian general staff. The sekretariat works constantly on the companies for which its bank is the hausbank and on the board of which one of the bank's executives sits. Since the bank also handles the commercial banking business of these companies, the sekretariat has access to both their financial and business data. There is no sekretariat in Japan. But the same function is discharged by the large and powerful planning departments of the keiretsu's main bank and of the keiretsu's trading company. They too have access to commercial and business data in addition to financial information.

Even the largest U.S. pension fund holds much too small a fraction of any one company's capital to control it. Law wisely limits a corporate pension fund to a maximum holding of 5 percent of any one company's stock, and very few funds go anywhere near that high. Not being businesses, the funds have no access to commercial or business information. They are not business-focused, nor could they be. They are asset managers. Yet they need the in-depth business analysis of the companies they collectively control. And they need an institutional structure in which management accountability is embedded.

In an American context, the business analysis—call it the business audit—will have to be done by some kind of independent professional agency. Certain management consulting firms already do such work, though only on an ad hoc basis and usually after a company has gotten into trouble, which is rather late in the process. The consulting divisions of some of the large accounting firms also perform business analysis assignments. One of them, KPMG Peat Marwick, actually offers a systematic business audit to nonprofit organizations, which it calls a resource-development system. And several firms have recently come into being to advise pension funds—mostly public funds—on the industries and companies in which they invest.

I suspect that in the end we shall develop a formal business-audit practice, analogous perhaps to the financial-audit practice of independent professional accounting firms. For while the business audit need not be conducted every year— every three years may be enough in most cases—it needs to be based on predetermined standards and go through a systematic evaluation of business performance: starting with mission and strategy, through marketing, innovation, productivity, people development, community relations, all the way to profitability. The elements for such a business audit are known and available. But they need to be pulled together into systematic procedures. And that is best done, in all likelihood, by an organization that specializes in audits, whether an independent firm or a new and separate division of an accounting practice.

Thus, it may not be too fanciful to expect that in ten years a major pension fund will not invest in a company's shares or fixed-income securities unless that company submits itself to a business audit by an outside professional firm. Managements will resist, of course. But only 60 years ago, managements equally resisted—in fact, resented—demands that they submit themselves to a financial audit by outside public accountants and even more to publication of the audit's findings.

Still, the question remains: Who is going to use this tool? In the American context, there is only one possible answer: a revitalized board of directors.

The need for an effective board has been stressed by every student of the publicly owned corporation in the last 40 years. To run a business enterprise, especially a large and complex enterprise, management needs considerable power. But power without accountability always becomes flabby or tyrannical and usually both. Surely, we know how to make boards effective as an organ of corporate governance. Having better people is not the key; ordinary people will do. Making a board effective requires spelling out its work, setting specific objectives for its performance and contribution, and regularly appraising the board's performance against these objectives.[3]

We have known this for a long time. But American boards have on the whole become less, rather than more, effective. Boards are not effective if they represent good intentions. Boards are not effective if they represent "investors." Boards of business enterprises are effective if they represent strong owners, committed to the enterprise.

Almost 60 years ago, in 1933, Adolph A. Berle, Jr. and Gardner C. Means published *The Modern Corporation and Private Property,* arguably the most influential book in U.S. business history. They showed that the traditional "owners," the nineteenth-century capitalists, had disappeared, with the title of ownership shifting rapidly to faceless multitudes of investors without interest in or commitment to the company and concerned with only short-term gains. As a result, they argued, ownership was becoming divorced from control and a mere legal fiction, with management becoming accountable to no one and for nothing. Then, 20 years later, Ralph Cordiner's *Professional Management* accepted this divorce of ownership from control and tried to make a virtue out of it.

By now, the wheel has come full circle. The pension funds are very different owners from nineteenth-century tycoons. They are not owners because they want to be owners but because they have no choice. They cannot sell. They also cannot become owner-managers. But they are owners nonetheless. As such, they have more than mere power. They have the responsibility to ensure performance and results in America's largest and most important companies.

Notes

1. This concept has long historical roots. The great English economist Alfred Marshall (1842-1924) first wrote of the "going concern" as the wealth producing entity in a modern economy of a hundred years ago. And the idea underlies the protection of the going concern (Chapter 11 bankruptcy) put forth during the New Deal into U.S. bankruptcy law. But as an operational guide to managing a business, maximizing the wealth-producing capacity of the enterprise has emerged only in the last 40 years.
2. C.K Prahalad and Gary Hamel, "The Core Competence of the Corporation," *Harvard Business Review,* May-June 1990.
3. The most thorough and persuasive analysis of what makes an effective board is a book by Harvard Business School Professor Myles L. Mace, *Directors: Myth and Reality* (Boston: Harvard Business School Press, 1986).

Index